Defending the American Family

the Pro-Family Contract with America

Defending the American Family

the Pro-Family Contract with America

by
Martin Mawyer

New Leaf Press

Dedication

To all the hardworking families in
America who have fought to return our
nation to its great heritage, timeless
beliefs, and cherished values.

Contents

Contents

1

A Troubled Nation

You all know about the famous Contract with
America — the pledge made to the American people in
the summer of 1994 by over 300 Republican congressional candidates. You've probably seen news clips of
the famous signing ceremony, held on the steps of the
Capitol. All the participants are dressed smartly for the
occasion, their faces grave. One by one they add their
names to the document, which many believe to be
historic in its implications for the future of our troubled
nation.

Those present — and the document they sign —
are preoccupied with the most important thing to many
members of Congress: economics, fiscal policy, and

money. And money is what the Contract for America is mostly about — taxes, the deficit, and other related issues. You can call it "congressional reform" or "fiscal responsibility" or "a break for the middle class," but in the final analysis the Contract assumes what too many politicians fervently believe — that the facts of life are economic, that if we solve our money problems, we will live in the Promised Land.

A healthy respect for money is admirable. Fiscal responsibility is essential to the survival of America's families. It is also of crucial importance at the national level. We can't manage our family checkbook one way and our government resources another, at least not for long. As recent events in Orange County, California, prove, governments can go bankrupt as well as families. So it's proper that the solemn souls signing this Contract for America represent all frugal people in cutting expenses and balancing the nation's checkbook.

But let me remind you of those who aren't represented in that picture or that historic document:

> • The teenage girls whose lives have been ruined because a Planned Parenthood counselor talked them into having an abortion,

> • The hundreds of thousands of people dead of AIDS because the government of the United States for the past 12 years has actively promoted the Gay Rights movement with tax dollars,

• The 75-80 percent of Americans who believe that God should not be barred from the nation's schoolgrounds,

• The lovers of painting and music and drama who have been offended by the subhuman works subsidized by the National Endowment for the Arts,

• The legitimate historians who don't equate history with propaganda and are therefore appalled by the politically correct "standards" funded by the National Endowment for the Humanities,

• The parents who are alarmed by the attempts of the U.S. Department of Education to set up a national curriculum to brainwash their children,

• The orthodox Christians and Jews and Muslims who don't want their tax dollars used to fund elitist radio and television broadcasts that attack religious beliefs and offend the sensibilities of millions of listeners and viewers,

• The parents who are tired of sending their children to a public school system that teaches disrespect for the traditional values taught in most families and churches,

• The growing number of babies born every year to unwed mothers.

Today congressional leaders repeatedly say they're worried about the problems of these missing people. But apparently they're too concerned with the budget and the tax burden to address these issues at the moment. In fact, there are times when these "moral" preoccupations seem to be no more than inconvenient distractions, irrelevant playthings to be put away in the toy box for a rainy afternoon.

Meanwhile, all the social problems of the country continue to multiply — not because government has done too little to eradicate them, but because government has done too much to promote them. Indeed, there is a government program fueling almost every social ill we now confront. The United States government is funding abortions, homosexuality, obscenity, illegitimacy, assaults on religion, programs that undermine the continued survival of the family, and the spread of sexually-transmitted disease.

This malicious meddling by the federal government must stop — and for at least three reasons, each of which should be persuasive enough to engage the attention of the Speaker of the House and his new Republican majority. Let's take a look at these three reasons in some depth.

Reason # 1. The Republican Party owes a debt to the pro-family movement. The time has come to pay that debt.

In November of 1994 the Republicans won an historic victory at the polls, capturing control of both the Senate and the House of Representatives. In so doing, they defeated the incumbent Speaker of the House, something that hadn't happened in more than 150 years. The Republicans had controlled the Senate during part of Ronald Reagan's presidency, but the last time they'd held a majority in the House was during Eisenhower's first term — 40 years earlier.

In part, the long reign of the Democrats on Capitol Hill was attributable to the support of blue-collar workers and their families — particularly Catholics and Evangelicals — who, under ordinary circumstances, tended to identify with the economic policies of the Democratic Party. Many were union members paid by the hour, and they believed congressional Democrats were sympathetic to the problems and needs of working people.

However, in the past two decades the Democrats have brought new interest groups into their coalition, activists whose agendas have offended the traditional sensibilities of many blue-collar workers. The feminists have too often promoted sexual license among women, maintained that marriage is a cruel form of bondage, and ridiculed mothers who remain at home to rear their children. Homosexuals have argued that the family is the source of hatred and bigotry, that the

Church has persecuted them for 2,000 years, and that homosexuals should be allowed to marry. The pro-abortion activists have opposed any form of restraint in this area, including a requirement that counselors inform parents before sending their minor daughters to an abortion clinic. The art activists have fanatically, unreasonably defended obscenity and attacks on religion, thumbing their noses at those who have asked for higher standards and tasteful restraint in the awarding of grants.

In the past several decades, these groups and their agendas have begun to dominate the Democratic Party; and many blue-collar families have consequently voted Republican, despite their historical predisposition to regard the GOP as the party of powerful, greed-ridden rich folks. In turn, the Republican Party has ostensibly supported pro-family values. The result: The Republicans have held the presidency for all but six of the last 26 years; and with the help of pro-family voters, they are now in control of Congress. Indeed, it is the so-called Reagan Democrats — most of whom are really "independents" — who have helped the Republican Party grow in size and power since the end of World War II.

So the time has come for the Republicans to deliver on their many promises to this constituency, to pay off debts they have incurred during the past several elections. They now hold strong majorities in both Houses, and they can force almost any measure to a vote and pass it, provided they all stick together. As yet, they don't have a sufficient number to override a presidential veto; but 1996 will afford them the greatest opportunity to consolidate their power since the early days of the twentieth century — *provided they are willing to deliver on the promises they've made in the past few years.*

The Contract with America, which occupied the first 100 days of the new Congress, contained many important and necessary items — the Balanced Budget Amendment, the Line-item Veto, reforms in the way Congress conducts its business, tax relief for the middle class, and an overhauling of the welfare system. Pro-family leaders have been supportive of these measures, willing once again — as in 1981 — to allow those interested in economic reform to come up to bat first.

Perhaps this was a mistake. Perhaps they should have insisted that the Contract contain all the major social issues as well as the Republican leadership's economic priorities. At this stage it's too late to speculate. However, pro-family forces and their supporters in Congress must step forward now and tell the Speaker of the House and the Majority Leader of the Senate that the social issues must be moved immediately to the front burner, that Republicans cannot expect millions of pro-family voters nationwide to be satisfied with mere rhetoric at a time when the feminists, homosexuals, and abortion advocates have already won so many signal victories.

Democrats have paid their debt to the anti-family constituency, risking the loss of millions of voters as a consequence of promoting the agendas of groups like the Gay Rights movement, the ACLU, the National Education Association, and the labor unions. The Democratic leadership has been true to its promises and has earned the trust and support of the hard Left.

The Republican Party cannot hope to hold power for long if it continues to neglect its pro-family constituency on the lean prospect that it will attract enough "moderates" from the Democratic Party to make up the difference. George Bush made that mistake and it cost him the presidency. If the Republican leadership in Congress doesn't "pay up" during this session, it may well find itself in the minority when Congress opens for business in January of 1997.

Reason #2. The moral problems we now face are related to the economic problems and are perhaps more crucial to the survival of the nation.

The two are so closely related that it's important they not be separated arbitrarily and artificially. What is moral and what is practical are occasionally oceans apart, but for the most part, traditional morality works in the real world, which is one reason why it has been around for so long. In this particular case, there are at least two ways in which the current moral climate adversely affects the world of taxes and deficits.

1. Immorality costs the government money.

Some of the most extravagant and durable programs funded by the federal government are designed to deal with the consequences of flouting the traditional moral code. The liberal establishment is telling the American people that they have no right to say what should or shouldn't go on in the bedrooms of private citizens. Yet if something goes wrong behind those closed doors — if an unmarried teenager becomes pregnant or one homosexual transmits the HIV virus to another — then the government orders the American people to pay for the consequences of irresponsible sex acts. Several examples come to mind.

Title X is a long-standing and costly program administered by the U.S. Department of Health and Human Services. One of its chief purposes: to take care of unwed mothers and their children. Nothing is wrong with such an impulse. Churches and other charitable groups have always been sympathetic with the plight of unmarried pregnant women and have provided homes and related services to ensure that they survive this difficult period in their lives. Whether or not the federal government should be engaged in such activities is a highly debatable question.

More to the point, the unintended consequences of Title X have been devastating, both in terms of billions spent and in lives ruined. For one thing, Title X has put the U.S. government in the business of subsidizing illegitimacy — and, as economists will tell you, you always get more of what you subsidize. Many teenage girls are delighted to learn that if they become pregnant Uncle Sam will set them up in their own apartment and pay their bills. For an adolescent girl who wants to escape the restrictive authority of her parents, an evening of illicit sex seems a small price to pay for what she views as "financial independence." As a consequence, hoards of unmarried girls actually seek to become pregnant at the earliest possible moment in their young lives. In fact, about 65 percent of all births to teenagers are now out-of-wedlock; and that figure has reached 92 percent among adolescent Blacks.

In addition to promoting illegitimacy, Title X is also supporting Planned Parenthood — an organization historically dedicated to the encouragement of early sexual activity and casual abortion. This group has sponsored some of the most outrageous sex education materials ever used to indoctrinate the young, and it is also the chief abortion provider in America. Each year Planned Parenthood receives tens of millions of dollars from Title X, enough to employ its sex educators and abortionists and fund their ugly activities. Without federal dollars, this organization would be severely crippled.

But Title X isn't the only government program that has spent huge sums of money on the consequences of immoral conduct. The Gay Rights movement, with its fierce commitment to promiscuous and perverse behavior, is costing the taxpayers more than a billion dollars a year just to deal with the AIDS epidemic. In fact, the federal government is now spending more money on AIDS research and treatment than on either cancer or heart disease, the top killers of Americans. In addition, hundreds of millions in tax dollars are also being used for "AIDS education," which is often nothing more than gay rights propaganda.

But the Gay Rights movement is also receiving funding from other agencies of the federal government, and encouragement from virtually all. Taxpayers are being asked to support "diversity training" in virtually all departments, which is little more than gay rights propaganda crafted to undermine the religious and moral convictions of federal workers and to compromise their consciences. Tax dollars are also being used for the development and promotion of "gay friendly" educational materials for use in the public school systems. And the U.S. Government Printing Office is publishing official "studies" that attack traditional religious beliefs and in some cases specific branches of the Christian faith. A staff member for a Republican congressman has prepared an 80-page report that documents literally hundreds of homosexual activities that are federally funded, some of them begun during the Reagan Administration.

So illicit sexual activity is a very expensive item on the federal tax bill, which means that the American people have a greater stake in maintaining traditional moral strictures than the media and liberal wings of both political parties would be willing to admit.

2. Moral decay undermines the nation's most important institutions and inevitably leads to fiscal irresponsibility and collapse.

The widespread use of drugs — a product of the new morality promoted in the 1960's — has proven disastrous to the stability of American society and to its most basic institutions. The drain on the nation's financial resources is ultimately immeasurable. One estimate places annual income from drug sales at greater than the combined profits of all the companies listed on the New York Stock Exchange. To put it another way, Americans are spending more on drugs than on any other product or service offered in the marketplace. This means that legitimate American business is losing an enormous share of its potential sales, that banks are losing incalculable amounts in potential deposits, and that the government is losing hundreds of billions of dollars in potential tax revenues. So the drug economy — built on a vice that has too often been romanticized by the Left — is the chief plunderer of legitimate profits and growth capital in this country.

In addition, drug use has become a way of life not only on the streets, but also in Wall Street brokerage firms and other financial institutions. The destruction of any incentive to do a day's work, the desperate need to get a fix, a drive that will impel an essentially honest human being to embezzle or steal, the destruction of family life that inevitably takes its toll at the office — these are a few of the problems that corporate America must face as the moral structure of society begins to fall apart at an ever-increasing pace.

In addition, corporations, like individuals, have had to pay a higher tax bill as a consequence of the additional expenses that widespread drug use incurs: the creation of an entire federal agency to handle the problem; the additional counselors and screening devices in schools; the exponential rise of drug-related crime, particularly among the young; the enormous cost of law enforcement; the loss to society of billions in income from potentially productive citizens whose lives have been ruined by drug use.

So it is impossible to separate what is financially responsible from what is morally responsible. We have attempted to separate the two for the better part of three decades now, and we are slowly, painfully coming to the realization that we can pass the Balanced Budget Amendment and still fall to pieces as a nation. That's another reason why we must realize that a genuine Social Contract with America is not just an inconvenient favor to religious America but an essential ingredient in the nation's survival kit. If we are to secure our financial future, we must first save the soul of the nation.

Reason #3. Supporting a Social Contract with America is the right thing to do.

Anyone who has spent a great deal of time around Washington is forever being invited to adopt an "inside the Beltway" attitude toward government. Don't worry about what's right. Calculate the odds for success. Figure the angles. Get in with the right crowd. Be prepared to compromise. Do what's practical.

With patronizing smiles, Washington insiders are in the habit of telling pro-family activists: "Politics is the art of the possible," as if they'd invented the phrase on the spur of the moment. Then they go on to teach a lesson of infinite patience and strategic retreat. As a matter of fact, several leaders of the most prominent pro-family, pro-life religious groups have fallen in with this line of thought, compromising their principles and those of their followers on the grounds that questions like abortion and gay rights are too divisive to bring up on the floor of Congress without threatening the success of such "important initiatives" as the middle-class tax cut.

As noted above, the pro-family agenda was put on the back burner in 1981, on the grounds that it had to wait while President Reagan fought for his tax cut and a reduction in government regulations and spending. "Just wait until the second term," the pro-family movement was told. "Then we'll push through major social legislation." Our pro-family leadership agreed; and as a consequence, our issues continued to simmer on the back burner, forgotten for the better part of eight years.

George Bush revived pro-family hopes briefly at the 1988 Republican Convention, promising, among other things, to promote tuition tax credits for parents who send their children to private schools. Shortly after he took office, Bush was asked by a youngster visiting the White House about this particular campaign promise. Crossing his arms before his face, like a movie heroine warding off a vampire, he told the questioner that, despite his campaign promise of a few months earlier, America just couldn't afford tuition tax credits. A few days later, a pro-family delegation went to see the president and came out of the meeting full of smiles. Their message to the general public: "We are very pleased with President Bush." As a consequence, nothing was done for another four years. In the 1992 election, Bush lost a substantial portion of evangelical Christians, enough to give the election to Bill Clinton.

We need not blame President Bush entirely for his lack of initiative, though he did break campaign promises to the pro-family movement. As we all knew, he seemed to be a politician who didn't feel strongly about the social issues. It was our fault — the fault of the pro-family movement — that we didn't force him to do better. We should have been more demanding, more adamant, more unforgiving of his failures. We should have let him know from the beginning that he could not count on our support unless he delivered the goods. Had we done so, he would have been a stronger, more credible pro-family president and probably would have been re-elected in 1992.

We should have pursued this line not because it was the most political course to follow, but because it was the *right* thing to do. Sometimes — more often than Washington gurus will admit — politics is the art of the *impossible*. Most of us who believe in God also believe in miracles. We see them in our own daily lives and in the lives of others — the unexpected transformations of the heart that turn doomed people into saints of the church. The same kinds of miracles occur in politics, and some of them are not supernatural transformations but the result of no more than perseverance and imagination.

In fact, those who oppose the pro-family agenda have often faced greater odds in the political wars than we have, because the American people are historically predisposed to look sympathetically on family life. Let me offer two examples of how the enemies of traditional values have overcome enormous opposition to advance their cause — because they did what they thought was right.

The first example is that of Madeleine Murray O'Hair, a solitary woman with neither a large organization nor partisan political support when she set out to remove prayer from America's public schools. From the founding of the nation, virtually everyone had assumed that states and localities had the right to sponsor a generalized prayer to begin the school day. Thomas Jefferson, in his second inaugural address, specifically addressed the issue, saying that the states retained these rights, had indeed brought them into the Union. In fact, until the 1960s, virtually every school in America allowed, even prescribed, some sort of prayer at the beginning of the day.

But Madeleine Murray O'Hair, an avowed atheist, objected to the practice and was determined to see it abolished. No one persuaded her to drop her campaign because it was "divisive" or "stirred up resentment" or interfered with other, more urgent programs. She didn't agree to postpone her agenda until the nation's economic problems were solved. With a single-minded devotion to what she believed was right, she took the American educational system to court and she won. In the wake of her victory, school administrators nationwide are clamoring to ban Bibles from school property, removing any hint of Jesus's birth from celebrations of "the holiday season," even challenging the teaching of sexual abstinence in our schools. All of this frantic renunciation of God has come about because one stubborn woman did what she believed was right rather than what seemed practical or even possible.

Now, when an overwhelming majority of the American people still believe that prayer should be permitted in public schools, faint-hearted politicians are telling us that we mustn't introduce such an amendment on the floor of Congress because it would certainly be defeated, either in the Senate or in the nation's legislatures. Clearly, they've forgotten the lesson of Madeleine Murray O'Hair.

As a second example of the impossible in politics, consider the success of the Gay Rights movement over the past two decades. Twenty years ago, the vast majority of Americans regarded homosexuals as either mentally ill or else deliberately perverse in their sexual behavior. Virtually all states had laws outlawing sodomy. Parents feared the presence of homosexual teachers in the classroom, since they knew instructors exerted a strong influence over youngsters, particularly smaller children. Homosexuality was almost never depicted in Hollywood films or on television screens; and when the subject came up on shows like "Marcus Welby, M.D.," gay characters were not depicted as either heroes or innocent victims of homophobia, but rather as sick or anti-social.

So at the beginning of the active "gay rights" movement in 1969, no one could have guessed that homosexuality would rack up such enormous gains in the 1980s. After all, Ronald Reagan was president and the nation was enjoying a conservative revival. Even more to the point, the AIDS virus surfaced just as Reagan was taking office; and at the beginning of the decade the disease was an almost exclusively gay phenomenon. Clearly, homosexuality was an unhealthy form of behavior, one that subjected its adherents to terrible risks — risks of disease and even death.

An objective observer in 1981 would have given the Gay Rights movement little or no chance of success. Rather, the climate suggested that homosexuals should not only put their agenda on the back burner, but perhaps return it to the deep freeze for 50 or 75 years.

Yet, facing the predisposition of a majority of Americans to look with disgust on homosexual acts and the numerous medical reports indicating that homosexuals are many times more likely to contract sexually transmitted diseases than heterosexuals, gay rights activists refused to despair in their quest for legislation granting them special rights and privileges. Instead of abandoning their agenda or compromising on principles in which they genuinely believed, the leadership of the movement plotted a strategy that actually used the AIDS epidemic as a means of gaining sympathy for their cause. Here are some of the things they've accomplished from the 1970s to the present.

• Using threats of boycott and physical intimidation, they forced the American Psychiatric Association to delete homosexuality from its list of mental disorders, despite the fact that a majority of dynamically oriented psychiatrists and psychoanalysts still believe that homosexuality is the product of dysfunctional family life and therefore a disorder curable through therapy.

• Using the same tactics, the Gay Rights movement forced television networks to give them the same status as Blacks, which meant that they were able to review all scripts touching on the subject of homosexuality and voice any objections. In other words, they won the right to censor television productions, which is why you see so many homosexual characters on television sitcoms these days, invariably depicted in the most flattering terms imaginable.

• Mainline churches, which once followed biblical teaching on homosexuality, are now ordaining homosexual clergy and seriously discussing the possibility of homosexual marriage.

• Perhaps most incredible of all is the success homosexuals have enjoyed in persuading or coercing school districts into instituting pro-homosexual curricula and learning materials. All over the country, youngsters are now being taught that homosexuality is "normal" and "healthy" and that 10 percent of the population is gay — none of which is supported by scientific evidence.

• Homosexual activists persuaded members of the Bush Justice Department to draw up and submit to Congress a "hate crimes bill," which, though camouflaged as a measure to protect other minorities, was actually designed to give homosexuals legal status as a protected group. The bill was passed by Congress and signed into law by President George Bush. His staff invited homosexual activists to the signing.

These extraordinary gains — achieved despite traditional moral and legal codes that condemned homosexuality, as well as rulings by the Supreme Court that anti-sodomy laws were constitutional — support the idea that those who fight for what they believe to be right often flout conventional wisdom and succeed beyond all expectations, even when they represent only a small minority of the population.

What a pity that, during this same period, pro-family forces — which have always represented the view of the majority — have chosen to be timid and conciliatory in their activities, reluctant to push their popular agenda while watching their enemies move aggressively to dismantle traditional institutions and to denigrate orthodoxy religion and its adherents. In some instances, the pro-family leadership has simply exhibited poor judgment, overestimating the strength of the opposition and underestimating the wisdom and virtue of the American people. In other instances, leaders have apparently lacked the courage to tangle with an opposition willing to go to any lengths to destroy traditional beliefs and practices. These opponents are fighting for a new and radically different social order. They are convinced their cause is just, that what they're doing is ultimately right. The pro-family movement must be equally principled, equally stubborn, equally willing to bear ridicule and abuse, equally eager to risk failure in order to gain the possibility of success. To do anything less would be to admit that our opponents are more principled than we are.

These, then, are the reasons why the Republican Party must sign a Pro-Family Contract with America, a legislative program that will discharge its debt to the pro-family community, strengthen the integrity of its initial Contract, and do what is right and best for the American people. The Pro-Family Contract must address not only the pressing need of the nation for a moral cleansing, but also the indignities that decent people have suffered because of the government's policy of promoting obscenity and perversity. The next 10 chapters of this book deal with the 10 promises the majority party must make if it is to redeem its pledge to reform government in general and the way Congress does business in particular. Briefly, these are those promises.

1. Pass a Voluntary Prayer Amendment.

The colonists declared their independence from

the English on the presumption that freedom is a gift from God. Since the earliest days of the Republic, our national motto has been "In God We Trust." The greatest leaders in American history — from George Washington to Abraham Lincoln to Teddy Roosevelt to Franklin Roosevelt to Ronald Reagan — have used the office of the presidency to affirm the importance of God in the public life of the nation. The U.S. Supreme Court has always begun every session with the prayer: "May God bless the United States of America and this honorable court." Yet small children may not pray in school because five ideological justices have so decreed in a ruling that shatters all legal and institutional precedent.

The ongoing consequences of this wrong-headed ruling have been devastating. Over the past three or four decades, the federal courts have taken "the establishment clause" of the First Amendment and turned it inside out. Where once it guaranteed religious liberty to everyone, in the hands of an ideological court it became the means of banishing religion from every nook and cranny of public life. Thus manger scenes and menorahs have been removed from public squares during religious holidays. Students have been forbidden to say prayers before class or to study the Bible on school property, and paintings of Christ have been removed from public buildings. In this manner, the First Amendment has become the scourge of religion rather than its defender.

Therefore, the prayer ruling, one of the great judicial errors of the twentieth century, must be reversed. Certainly the American people overwhelmingly support the idea that voluntary prayer should be permitted not only in our schools but in every phase of our public life. Yet no one has really mounted a serious legislative initiative to undo this terrible wrong. The time has come for such an amendment to be debated and passed by the Congress of the United States and sent to the legislatures of the various states for ratification. Who could doubt the outcome of this initiative? Who could question its political wisdom?

2. Eliminate all federal funding for the Gay Rights movement and other left-wing activists.

Many current political movements — and particularly those that promote far-out opinions and agendas — owe their very existence to federal funding. Some observers believe the Gay Rights movement would wither and die were it not for the enormous sums of tax dollars funneled to activist groups by various federal agencies. (Unfortunately, this practice has occurred during Republican as well as Democratic administrations.)

Such a gross misuse of government funds should offend the sensibilities of all Americans, regardless of their stance on the issues. The federal government must not use the tax dollars of Americans who oppose gay rights to fund the activities of those who promote such an agenda. The practice is not only unfair, but arguably illegal, since many of these groups lobby Congress in behalf of specific legislation. This principle should apply to organizations and groups that oppose the gay rights agenda — if, in fact, such groups are actually receiving federal funds. And groups promoting other issues and agendas should likewise be de-funded. Congress can easily pass a law to this effect, ensuring that those who oppose the principles of organizations receiving federal support can enjoy an equal opportunity to make their case to the American people.

3. Repeal Title X and end federal incentives to bear illegitimate children.

One of the few conservative ideas that liberals have begun to accept is the principle that the disappearance of the two-parent family in America is a major cause of social unrest in contemporary society. More and more people are now willing to say, "Dan Quayle was right! We must do something about illegitimacy." No longer is this cry merely an expression of moral outrage. It has become a social imperative. People who reject the Judeo-Christian sexual ethic still recognize the enormous value of growing up in a family headed by two natural parents who are married.

On the other hand, Title X, as noted above, is a program that actually encourages young women to bear children out of wedlock and to rear them in single-parent homes. The growing incidence of teenage pregnancy, out-of-wedlock births, sexually transmitted diseases among adolescents, juvenile crime, violent acts in our schools, and widespread drug use among our youth all point to the failure of this program to solve the problems it was created to address. Indeed, objective analysis strongly suggests that the point of view under-lying the program is the cause of the very ills it was supposed to help eliminate. The time has come to let young people know that the federal government does not favor sexual license and out-of-wedlock birth, if for no other reason than these things create social chaos and absorb substantial portions of the federal budget. Title X should be phased out as quickly as possible.

4. Abolish the National Endowment for the Arts and the National Endowment for the Humanities.

The National Endowment for the Arts should be eliminated for at least three reasons. First, it is an unnecessary extravagance at a time when we seem unable to balance the federal budget or reduce federal spending. Second, it presumes to "establish" one ex-ample of art as opposed to another, thereby putting the federal government's imprimatur on works whose es-sential worth is a matter of taste and opinion. Third, many of the projects funded by the NEA over the past decade have offended the aesthetic sensibilities of a large portion of the population and have attacked the religious views of the world's great faiths.

The arts flourished in America prior to the estab-lishment of the NEA. As a matter of fact, many critics would argue that the first half of the twentieth century produced greater poems, novels, paintings, musical compositions, and films than has the second half — and without the incentive of federal grants. The arts receive most of their funding from non-governmental sources;

and the argument that the NEA can "leverage" donations from private foundations and donors is simply another way of saying that the federal government is meddling in the art world, ensuring that the playing field is not really level. The Congress of the United States should abolish this agency.

The National Endowment for the Humanities has often (though not exclusively) funded esoteric research that has little or no relevance to the primary concerns of the American people. In its worse moments, the NEH has supported ideological projects designed to further the philosophy and agenda of those in power.

In an ideal world, someone should support the study of medieval alchemy and scholarly works on the essays of Emerson. However, the U.S. government should not take money from the pockets of wage earners to enable college professors to take time off from their teaching to prowl libraries and immerse themselves in ancient volumes, no matter how enlightening the resultant insights. Such projects should be supported by universities and private foundations.

On the other hand, the huge grant awarded to the development of "national history standards" was worse than irrelevant. It was an attempt to promote the incorporation of politically correct distortions into the curricula of the nation's schools. As such, this funding was not merely a waste of tax dollars but an attempt to pervert American education. This ideological study guide will haunt our schools for years to come. It is time to get rid of the agency that promoted such mischief.

5. Abolish the U.S. Department of Education.

The U.S. Department of Education was created by Jimmy Carter to pay off a political debt to the National Education Association. It was one of the larger mistakes of an error-ridden administration, a mistake that has cost the American people billions of dollars. Like all bureaucracies, it has grown like a virulent weed — sinking its roots deeper with every passing year, gobbling up more territory, increasing its budget, poking into areas that are none of its business. If we don't kill it now, it will soon be an ugly and permanent part of the political landscape.

Much of what the department does is useless. The gigantic Title I program, designed to improve the performance of slow learners in poverty areas, is well-intentioned but ineffectual. Taxpayers are spending over a billion dollars annually for an initiative that makes little difference in the lives of the children it is intended to serve.

But some of department's programs are actually damaging American education. Goals 2000, initiated by the Clinton administration, is calculated to impose educational reform from the top down, including the establishment of a national curriculum that stresses social revolution and political correctness. The department could be abolished without eliminating the few educational services the federal government should be offering, like the funding of research and the maintenance of educational statistics.

6. Pass the Human Life Amendment and stop the killing of the unborn.

The decision of five Supreme Court justices to overturn the majority of state laws and rule that abortion is a constitutional right ranks among the most outrageous abuses of power in the history of the nation. Most people believe that life begins at conception, because they are sensible human beings and know that any other explanation defies the laws of logic. English common law has always recognized the rights of the unborn; and even in the recent history of American jurisprudence, courts have awarded damages and determined cases on the premise that an unborn child is a person, a human being. Thus Justice Harry Blackmun's muddle-headed opinion on *Roe v. Wade* abolished reason and legal precedent and introduced an element of sheer madness into American courts.

This confusion must be remedied. We cannot allow five unelected officials to cast aside the wisdom of the ages and arbitrarily allow doctors to terminate the lives of unborn babies. This outrageous practice must be ended, if only because it has already led to further ethical problems involving the retarded, the elderly, and the ill. Life has been immeasurably cheapened by the events of the past two decades, and we must make certain that the nation atones for the crimes of the past by ensuring that future lives will not be taken arbitrarily, selfishly, and for profit.

7. Reinstate the full ban on homosexuals in the military.

Contrary to the claims of the Gay Rights movement and its supporters in the media, we have kept homosexuals out of the military for several reasons that have nothing to do with moral or religious objections, though these are by no means irrelevant to the question. First, any objective survey of the medical literature will reveal that homosexuals contract many times the number of sexually transmitted diseases than heterosexuals, in part because of the nature of their sex acts, in part because they are significantly more promiscuous. Second, placing homosexuals into military units introduces an element into the close quarters shared by soldiers, sailors, and marines that needlessly complicates military living arrangements. And third, historically, homosexuality has produced cases of "fraternization" — that is, intimate relations between commanders and those serving under them — that have significantly damaged military discipline and morale.

The current policy — which allows homosexuals to enter the military if they are "discreet" — solves none of these continuing problems. We must return to a stricter rule, one that will take into consideration the primary purpose of our Armed Forces, which is to defend the nation from attack by our enemies. Military service is not a right enjoyed by all citizens. There are rigid physical and mental requirements that prohibit many Americans from enlisting regardless of their sexual orientation. No one is arguing that those who are severely handicapped physically and mentally have a right to serve. Therefore, those who maintain that the ban deprives homosexuals of their civil liberties fail to understand the unique nature of military service in our society. Congress must step in and clarify the issue with legislation that excludes homosexuals from the Armed Forces, whether or not they remain in the closet.

8. Abolish the Corporation for Public Broadcasting.

The Corporation for Public Broadcasting (CPB) is the agency through which the Public Broadcasting System (PBS) and National Public Radio (NPR) are funded. In effect, PBS and NPR function as official government television and radio networks — using tax dollars, operating with the authority and prestige of the federal government behind them, free from the responsibility of competing with commercial networks. They can put on programs that offend or bore the majority of Americans without suffering the consequences, because their income is not based on their audience appeal, and they are not answerable to the public or to the public's elected representatives, except very indirectly. Congress can de-fund CPB, but they can't dictate policy. In this respect, like a handful of other government agencies, PBS and NPR operate outside the ordinary authority of government. The members of its board are appointed, but thus far that fact has made little impact on the programming of government-sponsored radio and television.

That programming has been both ideologically biased and offensive to the tastes of many Americans is a matter beyond dispute. The "news" and "public events" broadcasts have been aggressively left-wing, particularly during the Cold War; and in more recent years, PBS and NPR have promoted the feminist, gay rights, and environmentalist agendas in ways that have brought charges of distortion and misrepresentation from responsible critics, as well as from the general public. When PBS raises funds from the general public, they stress their children's programming, their productions of Shakespeare, "Masterpiece Theater," and William F. Buckley's "Firing Line," but they fail to mention the hard-left propaganda films and news broadcasts, the obscenity, the promotion of sexual perversion, and the anti-American bias that has characterized the liberal intellectual establishment since the 1960s.

The time has come to get the federal government out of the business of subsidizing partisan political commentary and obscene programming. Congress has no right to take money out of the taxpayers' pockets in order to promote ideas and values many Americans deplore. Let's give CPB the true freedom the agency really deserves — the freedom to compete in the free marketplace of ideas, without the heavy burden of a large federal subsidy. Let's give PBS and NPR the opportunity to fly on their own. Let's kick Big Bird out of the nest.

9. Abolish the office of the Surgeon General.

Taxpayers can no longer afford the luxury of supporting an office that performs no significant function and contributes to the high blood pressure of literally millions of Americans. Let's face it: For the past 15 years, the surgeon general of the United States has been nothing more than a windbag in a sailor suit. Dr. C. Everett Koop wrote a controversial report on AIDS that was full of information which he himself had to repudiate at a later date. Dr. Joycelyn Elders surprised the nation by making a greater nuisance of herself than Koop and by being wrong even more often. A woman both ill-informed and imprecise, she became the most embarrassing member of an administration full of outrageous figures.

Since the surgeon general no longer plays a directive role in the Public Health Service, the office should be abolished as quickly as possible, both to set a good example for other top-heavy government agencies and also to give the general public some peace. No one will miss the office. Everyone will be grateful for the savings, however small.

10. Pass a bill establishing a national databank to track child molesters and to hold full-scale hearings to determine effective strategies for the *prevention* of the sexual abuse of children.

The sexual molestation of children has become a national scandal. Few days pass without a breaking story of sexual child abuse — surely among the most disturbing crimes known to society.

So bold are pedophiles in the 1990s that they have formed a national organization and hold annual conventions. Too often the criminals who commit such acts move from city to city, region to region, repeating the same offenses, drawing minimal punishment, and then moving on to new territories and new victims.

While such crimes properly remain within the jurisdiction of the respective states, the federal government could render invaluable service to parents and law enforcement officers everywhere by keeping a complete and detailed record of all sex offenses committed against children and the names and current addresses of their perpetrators. Such a list would aid law enforcement agencies in moving swiftly after each reported disappearance of a child and also enable schools, day-care centers, and other organizations that work with children to prevent the hiring of known pedophiles by screening all job applicants.

These, then, are the 10 promises that signers of this Pro-Family Contract with America should make to the citizens of the nation — promises that they pledge to redeem by the end of the 104th Congress. Along with the enactment of the Contract with America, the fulfillment of these promises will justify the wisdom of the American people in deposing a tired and corrupt leadership and replacing it with a new team more in tune with the beliefs and values of the American people.

Of course, some critics are already charging that the sweeping reforms enacted will prove to be no more than small adjustments in the way Congress does business and a few cosmetic cuts to appease the more naive voters. But for the moment, the Republicans seem to have done a remarkable job during the first 100 days. They have accomplished a great deal more than the cynics believed possible when Congress was gaveled to order to begin the new session.

On the other hand, however well they've done on the Contract with America, the Pro-Family Contract remains — a necessary addendum to the 10 proposals of the original Contract. It's important to realize that, however controversial they may seem to the liberal establishment, the 10 promises of the Pro-Family Contract with America will be highly popular with the American people, who have indicated their support for most of these measures in poll after poll over the years.

To understand what is really at stake in these 10 promises, Americans should read very carefully the next 10 chapters of this book, which consider these issues one by one, focusing on the problems involved, exploring their intricacies, offering specific evidence to support the necessity for strong and immediate action. These are not issues that are peripheral to the debate over the future of the nation. In the minds of a substantial portion of Americans they lie at the heart of the struggle, overshadowing many of the economic concerns that have thus far occupied the leadership on both sides of the aisle.

Americans instinctively realize the soul of their nation — and not merely its economic future — is in jeopardy as the result of our current drift. Millions believe we stand on the brink of a moral bankruptcy far more destructive to our people than fiscal bankruptcy — and they believe that this Congress has the last, best chance to avert catastrophe. This book is an attempt to ensure that members of the House and Senate know precisely what's at stake and what they must do to redeem themselves in the eyes of pro-family Americans.

2

Stop Funding Abortion and Sex Education

Title X, which became law in 1970, is a government program originally designed to reduce the growing number of unwanted pregnancies, particularly among teenagers. It provides sex education to prevent pregnancies, abortions to prevent births, and care for a single mother and her child — or children. When this legislation was passed, its supporters made several assumptions about the nature of the problem they were attempting to solve.

(1) Those who supported the original bill believed that the main reason teenagers got pregnant was because they didn't know enough about sex and reproduction. Give them the kind of frank and explicit information they weren't getting at home and they would behave more responsibly and the pregnancy rate would decline.

(2) Title X's supporters also believed in the reliability of contraceptive devices and were convinced that if youngsters used condoms regularly, teenage pregnancy rates would drop even farther.

(3) Finally, the supporters assumed that sexual activity among teenagers was inevitable and that educational approaches stressing traditional morality and the wisdom of abstinence were doomed to failure.

These assumptions — and the legislation based on them — were both naive and cynical. They were naive because they reaffirmed the old heresy that education can save us from the frailties of human nature and that technology can solve all society's problems. They were cynical because they confirmed the twentieth-century notion that the sex urge is uncontrollable and that old-fashioned morality no longer appeals to smart, no-nonsense young people.

By the way, a principal instigator of this legislation was a Texas congressman who was then very active in the Center for Population Options and believed fervently in the gospel according to Planned Parenthood. He helped introduce the bill. He fought hard for its passage. His name was George Bush.

All three of the assumptions on which Title X was based have been proven false. Let's take them one at a time.

1. The Efficacy of Explicit Sex Education Stressing Contraception

Many researchers have evaluated sex education programs, most of them designed to prove that one approach is better than another. But the studies that shed the most light on the subject are those that (1) are sponsored by independent agencies rather than advocates and (2) deal with a large sample. Here are brief summaries of the best studies available on the subject, and they all come to the same conclusion: sex education programs that emphasize explicit knowledge and information on contraceptives — that is, the kind funded by Title X — *just don't work*.

• "Sexuality Education: A More Realistic View of Its Effects," by Douglas Kirby in *Journal of School Health* 55 (1985), 421-424.

One of the first advocates of sex education to sound a cautionary note about its extravagant public claims was Douglas Kirby. As far back as 1985, he was warning the health education community that contemporary approaches (i.e., detailed information about sex and about contraception) just weren't working as well as their promoters had maintained. His conclusion: "Sexuality education has been proffered as a partial solution to a variety of adolescent sexual problems. Research demonstrates that programs increase knowledge, but have little direct impact on values and attitudes, actual sexual behavior, use of birth control, and teenage pregnancy. The research shows that sexuality education programs are similar to other educational programs in their effects; many programs increase knowledge and a few help clarify values, but most probably will not have much influence on the direction of sexual values or on sexual behavior. Alone, they will not dramatically reduce unintended pregnancy."

• "The Effects of Sex Education on Adolescent Behavior," by Deborah Anne Dawson in *Family Planning Perspectives* 18, (1986), 162-170.

Writing in Planned Parenthood's house organ, a scholar in the field of sex education, drawing on her own doctoral research conducted at Johns Hopkins University, concluded: "Overall, however, the existing data do not yet constitute consistent, compelling evidence that sex education programs are effective in increasing teenage contraceptive use and reducing adolescent pregnancy. . . . Neither pregnancy education nor contraceptive education exerts any significant effect on the risk of premarital pregnancy among sexually active teenagers — a finding that calls into question the argument that formal sex education is an effective tool for reducing adolescent pregnancy."

• "The Role of Responsibility and Knowledge in Reducing Teenage Out-of-Wedlock Childbearing," by Sandra L. Hanson, Catholic University of America, David E. Myers, DRC, Alan L. Ginsburg, U.S. Department of Education, in *Journal of Marriage and the Family* 49 (May, 1987), 241-256.

Researchers for this study, funded by the U.S. Department of Education, derived their data from approximately 10,000 never-married females in the sophomore cohort of the nationally-represented "High School and Beyond Survey." This is an enormous sample for a sex education study, one of the largest ever; and its results are therefore worthy of serious attention. The conclusion of the investigators: "Results show that knowledge, as measured by sex education courses and self-reported birth control knowledge, has no effect on the chances that a black or white female will experience an out-of-wedlock birth as a teenager. However, when adolescents and their parents hold values that stress responsibility, the adolescents' chances of experiencing an out-of-wedlock childbirth are significantly reduced."

And what were the implications of this study for the future of the kind of sex education funded by Title X? Hanson, Myers, and Ginsburg spoke directly to that point:

> Our findings suggest that knowledge, as measured by birth control knowledge and sex education courses, is not successful in reducing the chance of out-of-wedlock childbearing.... These findings have important implications for programs and policies addressing teenage pregnancy and childbearing. Although sex education is often promoted as a way to reduce the incidence of early pregnancy, our results suggest that simply requiring more students to take more sex education, as it is currently provided, is not the answer.

• "Sexually Active Adolescents and Condoms: Changes Over One Year in Knowledge, Attitudes, and Use," by Kegeles, S.M., Adler, N.E. and Irwin, C.E. in *American Journal of Public Health* 78 (1988), 460-461.

This study, conducted in San Francisco, focused on the effect of AIDS information, including condom use, on 320 sexually active teenagers. Needless to say, by 1988 San Francisco was the "safe sex" capital of the nation, with information about condoms posted on billboards and buses, repeated on television and in newspapers, and taught in middle schools and high schools. The researchers found that teenagers received and understood the information but did little or nothing with it. Here is their summary: "In general, adolescents believed that condoms are effective at preventing STDs, with females showing an increasingly strong belief in this by the second interview. There was a consensus among both males and females that using a contraceptive that prevents STDs is of great value and importance. Importance rating decreased over the year among females. At both points of time females showed little intention to have their partners use condoms and were uncertain about whether or not their partners wanted to use them; they showed no change in these variables over time. . . ."

• "Schools and Sex Education: Does It Work?" by James W. Stout, MD, and Frederick P. Rivara, MD, MPH, in *Pediatrics* 83 (March, 1989), 375-379.

This article, published in *Pediatrics,* the official journal of the American Academy of Pediatrics, is a survey and evaluation of five studies published between 1980-1987. The authors chose "only those studies in which the effect of junior high and senior high school-based programs on adolescent sexual activity, contraceptive use, and pregnancy rate were evaluated." The authors' summary of their survey: "The literature was critically reviewed to determine whether evidence exists to support sex education in the schools as a method of altering sexual behavior, contraception, and adolescent pregnancy. Five studies were identified in which the effects of sex education on these outcomes were evaluated. The available evidence indicates that there is little or no effect from school-based sex education on sexual activity, contraception, or teenage pregnancy."

• "Changes in Acquired Immunodeficiency Syndrome-related Risk Behavior After Adolescence: Relationships to Knowledge and Experience Concerning Human Immunodeficiency Virus Infection," by Stiffman, A.R., Earls, F., Dore, P., and Cunningham, R. in *Pediatrics* (May, 1992).

This study dealt with precisely those students for whom current Title X programs are devised — inner-city adolescents and young adults at risk for HIV infection. The researchers tracked 602 subjects, focusing on changes in risk behavior, and the result of their study was a series of conclusions that should have put an end to any further commitment to a "safe sex" educational strategy. They found that: "knowledge about AIDS or HIV infection and its prevention was not associated with any change in risk behavior, nor were the number of courses of information about the epidemic, acquaintance with those who are infected, estimates of personal risk, or exposure to HIV-test counseling. In fact, youths whose risk behaviors increased the most were more likely to know someone who had died of AIDS and to estimate their own risk as high. Most youths reported that they did not use condoms regularly, disliked them, and had little confidence in their protective ability."

The conclusions they draw from these results are predictable:

Changes in preventive strategies and further research on the causes of behavior are needed . . . it is clear that knowledge does not improve risk level in this population, nor does exposure to counseling, experience with HIV-infected individuals, or awareness of one's own risk status. . . . The findings reinforce the results of other studies that find no association between knowledge and risk behaviors . . . It is apparent that neither information, nor the pertinence or relevancy of that information, nor various interventions are challenging youth's behavior. . . . *It is imperative to change directions quickly,* to find out what other aspects of the youths' lives might be preventing them from absorbing this information or might be predisposing them to receptivity so that they will change their behavior, and it is time to implement preventive interventions that focus on more than just presentation of information. . . . We must consider immediately implementing programs that will go beyond information dissemination and take into account known correlatives and causes of high risk behaviors" [emphasis added].

So much for the kind of sex education that Title X is supporting with tens of millions of tax dollars annually. Now let's consider the second assumption underlying the Title X agenda.

2. Condom use is an efficient strategy in preventing pregnancy.

During the same period that researchers were beginning to admit that explicit sex education was failing to make an impact on the problem of teenage pregnancy, others were revealing the fallibility of the condom, which — in the Age of AIDS — had become the contraceptive of choice, largely because of surgeon general C. Everett Koop, who claimed, in a famous report circulated widely throughout the United States, that condoms would "safely protect" both heterosexuals and homosexuals from the HIV virus. Here are summaries of a few of the many pertinent studies that disproved Koop's irresponsible claims.

- A study published in the *British Medical Journal* (July 11, 1987) revealed an alarming rate of slippage and breakage of condoms used by homosexuals in anal intercourse: One brand slipped off at the rate of 33 percent, one ruptured at a rate of 22 percent, and another at a rate of 20 percent.

- Also the distinguished British

medical journal the *Lancet* (December 21/28, 1985) reported the disquieting fact that in a survey of London prostitutes, researchers found that condoms broke up to 50 percent of the time during anal intercourse.

• On October 20, 1990, the *Lancet* published a letter from Rosemary Kirkman of the Family Planning Centre, University of Manchester, which read as follows: "I was surprised that in your September 22 note 'A good fit?' you reproduce the London Rubber Company's statement that 'most condom failure is due to incorrect usage,' without exercising the same critical evaluation that applies to the rest of your journal. We have shown that 52 percent of those who had obtained condoms from our family planning clinic had one or more either burst or slip off in the three months before our survey. As might be expected, regular users reported more accidents than occasional users, and I do not believe that most of these failures were due to snagging with finger nails, use of oil-based vaginal lubricants, or use of out-of-date stock.

I firmly support the general move towards the use of barrier methods of birth control; but we do the public no favour by promoting the idea among medical staff that it is all the fault of the user when things go wrong."

By 1987, even the dogmatic surgeon general was beginning to backpedal from the categorical statements he had made just a year earlier in his famous report, perhaps because numerous experts had warned the public that condoms were not so safe after all. Here are a few quotes, taken from a 1988 paper ("Will 'Safe Sex' Education Effectively Combat AIDS?") prepared by staff members of the U.S. Department of Education.

- Dr. Harold Jaffe, CDC's chief of epidemiology: "You just can't tell people it's all right to do whatever you want so long as you use a condom. It's just too dangerous a disease to say that."
- Dr. Theresa Crenshaw, immediate past president of the American Association of Sex Educators, Counselors, and Therapists, and member of the presidential AIDS commission: "If the wrong information is given, the effort will fail. It will *cause* death rather than prevent it. . . . Saying that use of condoms is 'safe sex' is in fact playing Russian roulette. A lot of people will die in this dangerous game."
- Dr. Bruce Voeller (president of the Mariposa Research Foundation,

which specializes in the prevention of sexually transmitted diseases) who was researching the effectiveness and durability of condoms: "The safe sex message just isn't true. You're still playing a kind of Russian roulette."

• Dr. Malcolm Potts, one of the inventors of condoms lubricated with spermicide, and president of Family Health International: "Telling someone who engages in high-risk behavior to use a condom is like telling someone who is driving drunk to use a seat belt."

If these statements weren't enough to cause Dr. Koop to trim his sails, the outcome of a federally-funded condom study should have completed his conversion. Commissioned to answer the questions posed by the AIDS epidemic, this study, conducted by researchers from UCLA, began in controversy and ended in disaster. First, American condom manufacturers attempted unsuccessfully to prevent the investigation of domestic brands and to force researchers to confine their project to foreign-made condoms. Then the research team had to break a vow of silence to warn the FDA that they had discovered in the marketplace a batch of "rogue condoms" that came apart in the hands of investigators as they opened the packages. The FDA looked into the matter and was told by the manufacturer that all the stock had been sold out. Two months later researchers found condoms from the same batch still on the shelves of Los Angeles drug stores.

Six months later the study came to an abrupt end. The federal government cut off funding for the project because the HIV infection rate was so high among Los Angeles homosexuals that NIH officials feared those participating in the study would become infected. Dr. Jeffrey Perlman was quoted in the *Los Angeles Times* (August 10, 1988) as saying:

> What has happened in the last two years is that gays in Los Angeles became supersaturated with the virus so that to [go ahead with] this study [would mean that] there is going to be a large proportion of the recruits who would have become infected. On that basis, it really came to an ethical question.

Dr. Perlman insisted it would be premature to say that condom use was futile in controlling AIDS:

> In a low-incidence area, you could say that condoms are almost foolproof.... In a place like L.A., in the gay community, one would really be talking about delaying infection rather than preventing it. I certainly didn't feel that this was true a couple of years ago, but I do feel it is true now.

Alan Parachini, the Los Angeles reporter who

broke the story, attempted to elicit a comment from Dr. Koop, but was told he was not available for comment. Later, when Congressman William Dannemeyer tried to question the surgeon general about his erroneous commitment to the condom, a furious Koop resorted to loud invective to avoid answering.

In fact, Koop, a proud and stubborn man unable to admit his error, led the entire nation down the wrong road like some crazed Pied Piper. The public health community in particular was hypnotized by the vision of the "condom as savior." Even as late as 1995, researchers were still trying to justify Koop's original act of faith.

In the January-February issue of *Sexually Transmitted Diseases,* Zenilman, and others, reported a new study of condom efficacy in preventing sexually transmitted diseases, using subjects who sought the services of STD clinics in Baltimore. The results:

> In the 323 male and 275 female (total = 598) subjects who completed a follow-up visit, 21 percent reported using condoms for every act of sexual intercourse over the previous 30 days; 21 percent reported occasionally using condoms; and 59 percent reported not using condoms. At follow-up, 21 percent of subjects had new incident gonorrhea, chlamydia, syphilis, or trichomoniasis. Fifteen percent of the men who were "always" condom users had incident sexu-

ally transmitted diseases compared with 15.3 percent of "never users;" 23.5 percent of women who were "always" users had incident sexually transmitted diseases compared with 26.8 percent of "never" users.

In other words, there was no statistically significant difference between the infection rate of "always users" and "never users." Yet instead of admitting that once more the condom had failed to measure up to its reputation, the researchers concluded instead that their subjects were probably lying.

This ostrich mentality is typical of those who worship at the shrine of the condom — and also typical of the supporters of Title X, who, over the years, have raised the funding for this program with unabated zeal, until in 1995 it is now approaching the $200 million mark. At the same time, another federal program — administered by the same office that managed Title X — was demonstrating the third fallacy endorsed by Title X supporters.

3. Sex education that emphasizes traditional values and abstinence won't work with today's youth.

While Title X was falling flat on its face, Title XX — a tiny program which at that time funded *preventive* programs emphasizing abstinence — was showing that sex education programs *can* reduce pregnancies and out-of-wedlock births, provided they teach traditional values and tell young people to postpone sexual activity. Apparently such an approach never occurred to the supporters of Title X, who continued — contrary to the research cited above — to push condoms into the faces of young people.

However, as a supreme example of the favorable research on "abstinence" education, Stan Weed and others of the Institute for Research and Evaluation, issued a major report entitled "Predicting and Changing Teen Sexual Activity Rates: A Comparison of Three Title XX Programs" — a 1992 study sponsored and funded by the Office of Adolescent Pregnancy in the U.S. Department of Health and Human Services. The study used information collected from more than 7,000 students, an enormous sample for a sex education survey. Second, the researchers collected data from the same students a year after the initial survey, an excellent means of checking and modifying initial results. Third, the research compared and contrasted three studies, two of them with a strict abstinence approach, the other utilizing a "values clarification" approach that encouraged students to make their own decisions. And fourth, the study was sponsored by the Department of Health and Human Services and therefore subject to rigorous scrutiny, particularly from bureaucrats supportive of "safe sex" education and hostile to the very idea of teaching abstinence. The result: the "strict abstinence" programs significantly affected the decision of teenagers to delay sexual activity and significantly reduced pregnancy.

This study was highly sophisticated in design and complicated in methodology, but the most important results are summarized in an executive summary. Below is that highly technical summary, followed by a translation.

Summary

The data demonstrated the relative impact that several different variables had on the dependent measures of intention to be sexually involved prior to marriage, and on the transition from virgin to non-virgin status during the period following the program. A student's *value system* is a strong predictor of both sexual intention and transition, and explains more of the variance than any other single factor. The *social system* (peer and parent factors) and *related risk behaviors* (i.e. alcohol and drug use, truancy, steady dating) are similar to each other in their degree of influence, and are a very close second to the value system with respect to relative impact. The *personality variables* (locus of control, need for affiliation and acceptance, future orientation, rebelliousness, perceived vulnerability, etc.) were more modest with respect to their relative influence, but still significant. Other research is cited which illustrates that the *information system* (knowledge about human physiology, reproduction) is the factor least likely to produce changes in sexual behavior.

Translation

This study demonstrates with a vengeance what the 1987 Hanson-Meyers-Ginsburg Department of

Education survey concluded — that the values young people (and their families and friends) hold — their ideas about right and wrong, good and evil — are the most relevant factors in determining teenage sexual behavior and that information about sex and contraception — the approach promoted in Title X — are of little or no utility. What students *believe* about sexual issues is the best predictor of the way they are going to behave, and what their parents and friends *believe* about these same matters is almost as important.

As for Title X, in the light of this research, you would expect a program based on such provably false premises to fall flat on its face, and that's precisely what Title X has done. By all measurable indicators the problems this legislation was designed to correct have ballooned since 1970 — teenage pregnancy, out-of-wedlock births, abortion, and sexually transmitted diseases. Consider the following statistics.

• *Pregnancies among teenagers have skyrocketed.* In 1972, two years after Title X went into effect, the pregnancy rate for teenage girls (ages 15-19) was 95.1 per thousand. By 1990, 20 years after Title X, that figure had climbed to 117.1. Statistically, this is an enormous increase.

• *Out-of-wedlock births have risen alarmingly.* In 1970, the rate of out-of-wedlock births per thousand among teenagers was 22.4. By 1992, it had *doubled!*

• *The number of abortions to teenage girls has also increased dramatically over the past two decades.* You would think that with the sharp rise in out-of-wedlock births, there would be correspondingly fewer abortions among teenagers, but the reverse is true. In 1972, two years after Title X, an estimated 191,000 teenage girls underwent abortion procedures. In 1990, that figure had risen to 350,970.

• Sexually transmitted diseases have become rampant among teenagers. Despite the fact that clinics funded by Title X screen for STD's and routinely hand out condoms, about 3 million teenagers contract one or more sexually transmitted diseases every year. In fact, for the first time in history, teenage girls have the highest gonorrhea rates in the country and teenage boys have the second highest. As a matter of fact, the rate among adolescent girls is 20 times higher than in women over 30.

There are a number of reasons given for these staggering increases, most of which can boiled down to a single reason: a general breakdown in traditional morality over the past three decades — a collapse so swift and so complete that older Americans are in shock. As for Title X advocates, they are in denial. They still believe that if you increase spending to provide more information, more condoms, and more abortions, sooner or later the problem will disappear, like the smile of the Cheshire Cat.

For this reason, over the years Title X has grown from a relatively small program — only costing $6,000,000 in 1971 — to a gigantic $149,585,000 in fiscal year 1992. The estimate for FY 1995 — **$193,349,000!**

Now let's suppose you were running a profit-making corporation to prevent the increase of teenage pregnancies, out-of-wedlock births, abortions, and sexually transmitted diseases — and that your company established the same record as Title X. Let's assume that your profits and losses are based on the rise or fall in these statistics. Several things immediately become clear.

> • Your company has lost money every year since 1970 — the time of its founding.
>
> • During the years you have experienced these steady, uninterrupted losses, your cost of running the company has increased enormously, exponentially — from a mere $6 million the first year to more than $193 million in fiscal year 1995.
>
> • Yet despite these extraordinary losses, you have not changed your initial assumptions about the nature of the mar-

ket in which you're competing and the product you're selling. Your course of action for the next 10 years? More of the same.

Of course, we all know that such a scenario is purely hypothetical — and for several reasons. In the real world, investors would not toss money into a venture without substantial market research indicating a high likelihood of success. Second, no board of directors would allow management to pursue the same failed policies for a 25-year period. After a year or two of losses, the board would have fired the management, brought in new blood, and insisted that the replacements come up with an entirely different policy for the company to follow. Third, no corporate managers or directors would sanction such wildly increased expenditures for such an unsuccessful venture. Rather than throw good money after bad for a quarter of a century, early in the game they would have insisted on reducing the budget and pursuing more modest goals, thereby cutting their losses.

Obviously the government and business operate in entirely different ways. Instead of abandoning a strategy that doesn't work, members of Congress have simply increased the funding for Title X over a 25-year period to the point where a minor program has become a big-ticket item in the federal budget. While $6 million is an inexcusable waste of money, $193 million is a scandal.

Yet, with the advent of the Clinton administration, the abstinence approach characteristic of Title XX was scrapped, and its programs are now indistinguishable from those of Title X — a triumph of left-wing ideology over scientific research and common sense. For this reason, both Title X and Title XX must be closed down. The federal government must abandon the sleazy business of telling young Americans that promiscuity is permissible and even desirable in a world of AIDS. The initial precept of the Hippocratic Oath is "First, do no harm." It's time Uncle Sam's doctors lived up to that oath.

3

Preventing Child Sexual Abuse

Perhaps there is nothing more insidious to the American family than molesters who roam our streets, churches, schools, neighborhoods, and businesses preying upon our children.

It used to be (and unfortunately, most of us still think this is the case) that child molesters were savages who picked up children at random by offering them candy or a ride in their car. And though the parent is still well-advised to instruct their children never to accept gifts or rides from strangers, this method of "picking up" children is rarely employed by the pedophile any longer.

The "modern" child molester is much more effective at seducing children without these strategies of old. And the reason is quite simple: Child molesters are better organized.

Today, pedophiles have formed such support organizations as the Rene Guyon Society, the North American Man/Boy Love Association, the Childhood Sensuality Circle, and others. They pass around newsletters, books, and post messages on computer bulletin boards. They share strategies, not only on how to seduce children, but how to disarm parents and even defend themselves from police if they ever get caught.

Through communication with each other, the pedophile has turned child molestation into a professional skill.

Rather than picking up a strange child off the street, child molesters now seek positions that place them near children: Youth clubs, day care centers, skating rinks, parks, schools, video arcades, malls, sporting leagues, churches, and many similar places.

There is no question (having investigated this subject in an earlier book), that child molesters have gained the upper-hand over parents, the police, and society-at-large. And one doesn't have to search far to discover why: The child molester is far more determined to get the child than society is at doing anything to stop them.

As mentioned earlier, parents still think of most child molesters as dirty old men in ragged trench coats who lurk in dark alleyways or cars. Unwilling to educate themselves about how pedophiles really work, parents resort to teaching their children only the basics about protecting themselves — such as not accepting gifts or rides from strangers, and perhaps about "good touches and bad touches." But the typical child molester could care less about these warnings.

Child molesters know that parents tell their children not to accept gifts from strangers. That is why most have abandoned this strategy and now seek positions where they can befriend the child — and befriend the parent — so that they are no longer an outsider. And if a parent tells a child not to talk or go off with strangers, then the molester will dress up as a police officer, nurse, doctor, or some other authority figure.

If the child is told about "good touches and bad touches" then the molester will show a child "adult" pornography and "prove" that these touches are really good touches, not bad. He'll point out that the adults are smiling in the pictures, that they're having fun and obviously *not* being hurt. He'll then ask the boy or girl whether they have ever accidentally seen, or otherwise been told, that their parents do the same thing. He'll then instruct the child that these touches are really how people show love and affection toward one another. To complicate this even further, the molester will rub the genitals of the youngster and ask whether it feels good or bad. The molester knows, that in most cases, the physiological sensation will feel good.

In other words, for every *simple* answer parents and society develop for fending off the child predator, the molester can overcome it with a *simple* solution.

In another instance, child molesters know that it

is very difficult to pick up a child who has a strong relationship with his or her parents. And, quite frequently, the molester is looking for children from poor family environments. This is why a pedophile will often "screen" a child before making any further advances. They'll ask the potential victim such questions as, "What are the names of your parents?" "Where do they work?" "What do they do with you on the weekends?" "What's your address and telephone number?" and "Does dad play ball with you?" But parents are badly mistaken if they believe it's only children from poor family relationships who are abused.

Since child molesters exist everywhere, big cities and small towns, the pedophile has a strategy for every situation. If a molester lives in a town where he believes family relationships are good, then the pedophile will seek a position that can easily disarm the parent. A church leader, for example, is not only an acceptable position, but one that is highly attractive and frequently chosen. As one child molester (thrice convicted) told me, "Churchgoers are gullible. I've met many children this way."

The strategy for churches (as with any club, school, or youth organization we place our children into) is for the molester to be in a position that *compels* the parent into a trusting relationship. I use the word "compel" because the nature of the job itself is one of trust with our child. We place our children into the hands of youth ministers because we trust them for our child's spiritual well-being. We place our children into the hands of teachers because we trust them for our child's educational future. We place our children in the hands of youth sporting managers because we trust them for our child's athletic skills.

In these positions, the child molester doesn't have to *earn* our trust. Instead, our trust is given over as soon as we turn the child into his or her care. The molester understands this, which is why this strategy is so much more effective for picking up children than offering them free rides or gifts. In these positions, the molester not only quickly earns the trust of the child, but the parent as well. And what makes matters even worse is that we, as parents, are dropping our child off at the molester's doorsteps. In this age of the "modern" pedophile, the molester is oftentimes not coming *after* our children; instead, we're *bringing* our child to them!

Another misunderstanding among parents, police, and society-at-large is the universal view that pedophiles are "part-time" child molesters. This mistaken view has led many a police department to ignore the activities of *convicted* and *known* child molesters in their communities. It has led many a court to let child molesters *go free* without so much as a slap on the hand. And has led *most* parents to ignore trying to understand this problem so that they can better protect their child.

The typical child molester is a "full-time" operator. They seek jobs near children. They seek homes near schools. They hang out in video arcades, malls, and skating rinks. They seek volunteer work with youth organizations. Their private time is spent reading child pornography, talking to other pedophiles on computer bulletin-boards, or studying new strategies for seducing children. Between *these times,* they are courting their next victim. As alarmist as this sounds, these are the facts society has failed to realize. And it's no wonder that one child molester told me that finding a child to molest is as easy as "going to a refrigerator door and getting food out."

Without a proper understanding of this problem, society and parents will continue to devise failed solutions. There's no question that parents and schools, for instance, may feel good that we are doing *something* to protect our children by teaching them "good touches versus bad touches" and staying away from strangers for instance. But for as good as we may feel for having done something, our strategies for battling this epidemic are equally as worthless.

This is why, year after year, regardless of our recent fad-solutions for solving this problem, the number of child molestations keep increasing, as well as the number of child abductions for sexual purposes.

During the past 10 years, it has become obvious that society wants to deal with this problem. But when experts look at the solutions being offered, it also becomes obvious that society doesn't really want to understand the problem. Some judges, for instance, are beginning to take a harder approach with convicted child molesters and are beginning to send them to jail. (Previously, judges looked upon child molestations as "victimless crimes," because both the child and his molester were consenting partners, and the molester rarely went to jail.) But as more and more molesters go to jail — and get out — these molesters are becoming

more and more violent with their victims. The reason is
that convicted molesters (who oftentimes have to be
segregated from the rest of the prison population for
their own protection) don't *ever* want to go back to jail.
So they determine within themselves that the next child
they suspect will tell on them, they will either injure as
a reminder to keep silent, or kill to prevent the incident
from ever being disclosed. Now, if you combine this
problem with parents who tell their child the difference
between "good touches and bad touches" and that they
should not let *anyone* give them a bad touch, then that
child is in more danger of being injured — and even
murdered — than a child who does not resist his
attacker.

Failing to first understand the problem before
constructing solutions, therefore, presents additional
dangers to our children.

There *are* many directions which parents can
take and society as well. And they are outlined in my
previous book, *Silent Shame: The Alarming Rise of
Child Sexual Abuse and How to Protect Your Children
From It* which is available through the Christian Action
Network.[1] But this chapter is written to explain what
our federal government can and *should* do.

A universal strategy among child molesters who
get caught, is to change locations, dupe a new community, fool a new set of parents, and work their way into
new positions that afford them easy access to children.
This is easily done because it's difficult to track the
conviction records of known child molesters.

The federal government needs to establish a

national computer system for registering convicted child molesters. This system should be accessible by local police (to prevent unauthorized abuse of this information), but available for any business or group which deals mainly with children. Oddly enough, a day-care center, for instance, can spend a couple of dollars to check an applicant's driving record with the motor vehicle department, but these same child-care providers cannot, with any degree of accuracy, check to determine previous convictions for child sexual abuse. Day-care providers, schools, youth clubs, and others working with children should know whether they are hiring a convicted child molester.

Congress should provide funds for the FBI to conduct training seminars for local police on how child molesters operate. The FBI has gathered, cultivated, and researched the problem of child molestations beyond comparison. But filtering this information down to local police has been crude and restrained, at best. Child molesters, for their part, have freely passed their own strategies on to each other. These strategies not only include how to seduce children, but how to fend themselves from the police. They call it the "sympathy game," the "sick game," and the "blame others game." But the FBI, primarily due to lack of funds and congressional authority, has had little success in passing their information down to local law enforcement officials.

For more than a decade now the FBI has been studying this problem. They have profiles on virtually every type of pedophile that exists: The "Closet Pedophile," the "Cottage Pedophile," the "Isolated

Pedophile," the "Commercial Pedophile." They have profiles on the "Typical Child Molester" — his age, dating habits, buying habits, and more. And beyond this, the FBI knows how child molesters network together across state lines for the seduction of children, both for personal *and* commercial use.

This information, and more, needs to be presented in seminars to local police departments in every community. And the FBI should routinely update these seminars as it gains new information. The average police department in this country consists of less than 10 officers. It is understandable, therefore, that the FBI (which has far more funding and resources) is better educated on the nature and causes of sexual exploitation than local police departments. Nevertheless, child molesters live in communities — not on federal property. If Congress is truly concerned about preventing child sexual abuse (rather than simply figuring out ways to punish the offender after the crime has been committed) then they should authorize the funding and enabling legislation to provide for these training programs.

Congress should set stiffer sentences for child molesters and for those who abduct children. The reason a number of bills have continually been introduced in succeeding Congresses calling for stiffer sentences is because so many child molesters walk free. In fact, even the bills calling for *stiffer* sentences typically call for only three years imprisonment. The fact that *three years* is viewed as a *stiffer* sentence is a ringing commentary on how easy the courts *are* on convicted child molesters. Some readers are probably reminded that it used to be a capital offense to commit rape and to kidnap a child. These same readers probably also remember that there used to be fewer instances of rapes and kidnapping when these crimes *were* capital offenses. Personally, I'm uncomfortable with sexual molestation being a capital offense, but only because I know that so many *false* accusations have arisen in recent years by children. And I am also aware that too many prosecutors and youth counselors convince children they *were* sexually abused, even when they were not. But stiffening the penalties for convicted child molesters is a necessity and any legislation mandating that convicted molesters go to jail is better than the current system in most communities.

Regarding the abduction of children, however, a capital offense should be reinstated. I can imagine no greater nightmare (even the death of a child) than to have one's child abducted. In most cases, these children are never returned home and are oftentimes used for commercial purposes.

A former FBI assistant director, Lee Laster, has explained, "Kids *are* being passed around. The child pornography filmmaker in Queens (New York) knows a guy in Chicago doing the same thing, or in Los Angeles doing the same thing. In fact, there may be instances where there's a child that's done good in a film there and they ship the child somewhere else to make a film. In state hearings in New York City there is testimony that some pimps are shuttling young kids from one city to another. They can make a boy available for a party, for a weekend, or a week, or on a *permanent* basis if they want. Do you want a film, picture, or prostitute? If you know the right phone number, that's not a problem."

Most often the abductor molests the child for a period (until the child is no longer the desired age) and then dumps the child back on the streets. These youngsters, having long forgotten their true homes, and having been used solely for sexual purposes, become child prostitutes in major cities throughout the country.

And the parents *never* see their child again.

Congress should conduct full-scale hearings on the *prevention* of child sexual abuse. On April 4, 1995 the House of Representatives passed a bill called the "Sexual Crimes Against Children Prevention Act of 1995." There was nothing, however, in this bill that would help *prevent* child sexual abuse, even though it was so labeled. Primarily, the legislation mandates tougher sentencing guidelines for convicted child pornographers and certain molesters. This may be fine and well, but it still has nothing to do with prevention. Even more significant, the House of Representatives never held hearings on the bill to determine the actual effect this legislation would have on the problem.

Again, what became quite evident with the passage of this bill in the House is that members (as parents) want to do something about the problem, but — on the other hand — they don't want to understand what the problem really is.

Members of Congress take up the issue of child sexual abuse primarily because of personal or political reasons. They feel revolted at the thought of a child being sexually abused (personal) or they couldn't possibly explain to their constituents why they voted against a bill to punish child sex offenders (political). These two reasons alone will guarantee the passage of almost any legislation calling itself the "Prevention of Child Sexual Abuse."

Nevertheless, Congress needs to go beyond their personal and political motivations on this issue. They need to hold full-scale hearings and talk to experts and professionals in this field and finally develop effective measures for preventing child sexual abuse. Understandably, Members don't want to really know the disgusting, heart-breaking, obscene and tragic details regarding child sexual abuse. But then again, neither do the police investigators and the FBI agents who must work in this field — but they do it anyway, because it has to be done. So should Congress.

Only by talking to experts will Congress understand some of the difficulties of the legislations being offered. If, for instance, Congress feels led to pass a "three-strikes and you're out" law (that is, a law mandating life in prison after the third conviction) then Members need to know the implications this will have on child sexual abuse. Experts in this field are well aware that many child molesters will kill their next victim to avoid their third conviction. The reasoning behind this is because the child molester is going to spend life in prison anyway, so why not kill the child.

Congress also needs to understand why training seminars are important for local law enforcement officials. Few members of Congress, if any, are aware that many child molestation cases go unprosecuted because police officers are not trained in this area. For example, officers are reluctant to prosecute child pornography cases when the pictures depict children who are smiling or when the perpetrator is not making money on the films or pictorials. They feel these would be hard cases to win. In fact, they're not. Other police officers are reluctant to prosecute cases involving alienated children who come from rough backgrounds, as though the laws only protect children who are sweet and innocent. There are reasons why the alienated child is more vulnerable to sexual exploitation than other youngsters, but law enforcement officials are ignorant as to the causes. Another problem facing local police departments is what to do about children molesting children. More and more frequently the perpetrator of sexual abuse is a child as well — an 11 year old, for example, molesting a 2 year old.

The Federal Bureau of Investigation is not only aware of these problem cases and how best to proceed in their prosecution, but can also inform police departments how child molesters operate. Currently, the FBI holds between one and two training seminars a year (in Quantico, Virginia), which is in a small facility holding only 20 attendees. To complicate this matter, few police departments have the resources to send their officers for this specialized training. Only by holding full-scale hearings can these problems be brought to Congress in hopes of constructing a solution.

Congress should also hear the problems associated with the creation of a national computer databank of convicted child molesters. The primary problem is who should be placed on the system. Virtually everyone would agree that a 35-year-old man molesting an 8-year-old girl should be placed on the databank. But what about a 19-year-old man who had sex with a 16-year-old girl? Should that person be branded as a child sex offender for the rest of his life?

It might also come as a surprise to Congress that many child molesters are not convicted on actually having sex with kids. Instead, they plea bargain their case down to a trespassing or forgery conviction. Is it possible to place these cases on the databank? If so, what are the chances of abuse or mistakes being made along the way? It would be a crime in itself to mistakenly place a trespasser on a databank of convicted child molesters.

Congress is also unaware that the average length an FBI investigator remains in the child sexual abuse field is less than two years. This is partly because of the investigator feels maligned from having to search through wretched material, day in and day out. But it is also because the job has a low status within the FBI. Could Congress establish routine commendations for these investigators to be handed out by the attorney general, or even the president? What other incentives can Congress offer to keep these investigators in this field, such as increased salaries? The high turnover rate within the FBI has caused many officials to feel they are having to re-invent the wheel on child sexual abuse investigations every two or three years.

The problems raised here are not to suggest that there are no solutions. For example, having the computer databank register only those who are convicted for the specific crime of sexually abusing children — and perhaps for only those who have been convicted twice — would certainly solve many of the problems raised, and such a system would be far better than what's being offered now, which is nothing.

The purpose of raising these problems is to prod Congress into considering two issues: (1) that true prevention of child sexual abuse is more than simply stiffening the sentences of convicted molesters and (2) that Congress needs to hear from experts and professionals in this field to explore both the benefits and dangers of the various legislations being offered.

Significant results in the area of child sexual abuse can be made, but only when Congress approaches this territory with an open-mind about its solutions — which is rarely the case. Personal and political motivators to do something are fine and necessary. But such motivators should lead to effective solutions, which can only be constructed when Congress takes the time to delve into the world of the child molester. Fortunately for Congress, there are enough investigators and experts who have already done this for them. Now the question remains: Will Congress take the time to hear what they have to say — not just about what Congress wants to do, but what Congress should do?

4

Abolish the Department of Education

Many Americans forget that the U.S. Department of Education — which has drawn so much flak recently for its attempts to nationalize curriculum — is less than 20 years old. Created by Jimmy Carter as a payoff to the National Education Association, it is an agency we didn't need, a department that should never have come into being. As a matter of fact, federal funding of education is a relatively recent phenomenon, begun only about three decades ago on the assumption that money could solve the relatively minor problems facing our schools at the beginning of the 1960's. The major problems developed about that time. Some experts maintain the two events are connected.

One thing is certain: Federal initiatives designed to improve education have failed to eliminate the deficiencies they were established to address. Let's take a look at the three most ambitious programs operated by the U.S. Department of Education and see what has happened to them over the years.

The Guaranteed Student Loan Program

The largest boondoggle administered by the Department of Education is the Guaranteed Student Loan program, which costs taxpayers more than a billion dollars every year. In addition, it has driven up the price of a college education to the point where even middle-class parents have a hard time paying for tuition, room, board, and books. The result is a financial crisis in education the dimensions of which the general public has yet to grasp fully.

Like many federal programs, the original purpose of the Guaranteed Student Loan program seemed worthy, and the risk minimal. Here's how it was supposed to work:

> • The United States government would guarantee loans to needy students for tuition and other college expenses.

Banks would lend students the money at low rates. The students would use the money to earn a college degree or learn a trade at a vocational institution.

• As a consequence of this additional education, students would be able to get better jobs and take home a larger paycheck. With this solid income, they would be able to repay their guaranteed loans over a reasonable amount of time without straining their budgets.

• The program seemed foolproof, a scheme which would transform everyone into a winner. The college or trade school would get more students and hence increased tuition revenues. The bank would be able to make risk-free loans. The federal government would reap future rewards in taxes paid on incomes substantially greater as a consequence of higher educational achievement.

• This was the rosy picture that Congress painted in passing the original authorization for the program and appropriating the money. But the results have been anything but rosy. Indeed, the program has proven to be a disaster. Everyone except the banks and a few fly-by-night hustlers turned out to be a big loser.

• As soon as the word got out that Uncle Sam was throwing money at higher education, a number of promoters set up "proprietary schools" to teach students marketable trades and skills. Unlike the many legitimate institutions, these phony schools took the money the students borrowed and gave them useless training — or no training at all.

• When these students tried to find jobs, they found they were unqualified and that their diplomas or certificates were worthless in the marketplace.

• Without decent jobs, students were unable to repay their loans. And many who were able simply refused to do so on what proved to be the sound premise that the federal government probably wouldn't come after them anyway.

• When the students defaulted, the banks came to the Department of Education and the government had to make good on their guarantee. The result — literally billions of dollars shelled out to cover student defaults.

Only in the past few years has the Department of Education begun to address the problem. But at what cost? With a more aggressive collection policy, the feds are beginning to recover some of the lost funds. Belatedly, students are now required to pay up — in some cases when the training they bought was worthless.

In the meantime, billions of extra dollars in the

academic marketplace have created an inflated economy. Colleges and universities have expanded their own bureaucracies, knowing that Uncle Sam will supply whatever additional funds are necessary to meet rising tuitions. Unfortunately, in the process, educational institutions are now hooked on federal dollars. Most smaller institutions would fold if they were suddenly told that their students could no longer receive loans.

This excessive dependency on government-insured loans has in turn jeopardized the academic freedom of many colleges and universities. In slightly simplified terms, here's how.

• In order to ensure the quality of academic institutions and advanced training programs, the federal government had to find some method of determining the viability of every institution eligible to benefit from the student loan program. Since the Department of Education couldn't possibly investigate the thousands and thousands of institutions involved, experts decided to let the various accrediting agencies police the institutions for them. The Department would simply decide which accrediting agencies were reputable and "recognize" their members as institutions that students with guaranteed loans could attend. This strategy, everyone believed, would solve the problem. In fact, it simply posed additional problems.

• Some established accrediting agencies soon realized that they now had the power of life and death over their member institutions. If the agency withdrew accreditation, the school would immediately face an insurmountable financial crisis, one that few could survive.

• Armed with the power of life and death, two regional accrediting agencies began to interfere in the internal management and academic planning of member institutions. Middle States told one conservative seminary it had to place a woman on its board, despite the bylaws of the college which stipulated that the trustees be clergy (the denomination only ordained men). Western States passed new guidelines that mandated a multi-cultural curriculum, thus jeopardizing the program of Thomas Aquinas College, which is well-known for its "great books" program, which teaches the works of "dead white males."

• Because he understood the threat to academic freedom, Secretary of Education Lamar Alexander fired a warning shot across the bow of accrediting agencies and they backed down. But under another Secretary, the Guaranteed Student Loan program could be used to capture and restructure higher education in America along politically correct lines.

Unfortunately, too many people are now dependent on the GSL program to close it down immediately. Students and their parents routinely plan on the use of government funds to finance higher education. At some colleges and universities, more than 80 percent of enrollees are relying to some degree on Uncle Sam to pay their bills. The banks are as happy as clams over the arrangement. It will be a long and difficult process to break the habit, something like getting off crack cocaine after a five-year addiction. But somehow it must be done — and we should begin by closing down the agency that has made such a mess of a good impulse.

Title I

Another humanitarian impulse gone awry, the Title I program was devised to help "at-risk children" improve their academic performance. Special teachers, paid out of federal funds, were installed at schools located in districts where income fell below the poverty level. Experts were imported. Technology was supplied. This program eventually cost taxpayers more than $1 billion annually, and the department's own evaluation has demonstrated that it is a failure, that the performance of "at-risk" youngsters has not improved during the years Title I has been in full swing. Yet this program has also become a sacred cow because its original intent was praiseworthy.

At some point, good intentions no longer justify

an expenditure that has added measurably to the deficit — and an ineffectual program that costs over a billion dollars each year is measurable by anybody's standards. Again, the best way to terminate the program is to terminate the agency that administers it. Unlike the GSL program, Title I is non-addictive. Many school administrators resent the paperwork and would just as soon see the program abolished and the Title I teachers walk off into the sunset. Others shrug their shoulders and say it doesn't matter one way or another. To be sure, some will argue in favor of retaining the program, in part because they would like to believe in the tooth fairy and in part because schools receive a small portion of the allotted funds.

Goals 2000

This program, instituted by the Clinton administration as the Democratic answer to America 2000, is an attempt to restructure American education at the federal level by using the developing national standards in both curriculum and teacher training and certification.

The strategy: Give states and school districts federal dollars, provided they are willing to do what Goals 2000 prescribes, which is nothing less than the establishment of a politically correct curriculum to mold the thinking of our young people. The result: widespread revolt among parents nationwide and the emergence for the first time in history of a national movement to recapture control of the schools from the ideologues running it. As a matter of fact, there is every reason to believe that we can reverse the trends of the past thirty years and return our schools to a sound educational approach, one that stresses discipline, academics, and the basics.

But one of the greatest barriers to the reemergence of traditional educational values is the influence of federal funds on local school districts. In Ohio, parents trying to fight a particularly insidious form of indoctrination on sexual matters were told by members of the Ohio Department of Education that unless the state adopted federal health education guidelines — stressing condom use and tolerance for homosexuality — "needed" federal funds would be withheld. How much easier it would have been for parents to pursue this struggle had there been no U.S. Department of Education, no national "guidelines," no bribe to state and local schools.

Some people have argued that Goals 2000 is nothing more than a way of getting everybody involved in the improvement of education, that it is as innocent and benevolent as a church picnic. "All we're trying to do," its defenders say, "is to get folks together so we can all work to make our schools better, and help our children to compete in the world marketplace by the year 2000. How could anyone object to a little cooperation in behalf of learning?"

But of course more — much more — is at stake. If you don't believe the program's attackers when they tell you this is a federal grab for the entire educational system in America, then listen to what its proponents have been saying.

• The Department of Education — in its "Justifications of Appropriation Estimates to the Congress Fiscal Year 1996," Volume I — said the following: "The enactment of Goals 2000: Educate America Act and the School-to-Work Opportunities Act signaled the beginning of a new era in education reform that *will over time touch all schools.*"

• John F. Jennings of the Institute for Educational Leadership, saw the beginnings of the federal power grab in the Bush Administration's educational initiatives. Of America 2000, the Bush plan, he wrote: "It was a self-proclaimed conservative Republican . . . who was advocating a monumental movement away from local control of education."

• Albert Shanker, head of the American Federation of Teachers, said of Goals 2000: "[It's] the most important education legislation we've ever had." The significance of this statement is apparent when you realize that the unions considered federal aid to education and the creation of the U.S. Department of Education monumental steps in the right direction just a few years ago. Now one of their leaders is saying that the Clinton administration's program is even more important than these earlier breakthroughs.

• The Council of Chief State School Officers is an organization that coordinates the activities of state superintendents of public instruction, educational commissioners, and others who head state school systems and state boards of education. Though some of the "chiefs" are politically and socially conservative, a majority are probably to the left of center, and their national office in Washington is among the more left-wing activist groups in the nation's capital. Gordon M. Ambach, Executive Director of the organization, has said of the Clinton program: "In the first three titles, Goals 2000 establishes overall direction for a new local-state-federal partnership in education."

• Jennifer O'Day, the associate director of the Pew Forum on Educational Reform, says the legislation breaks new ground and sets remarkable precedents: "Perhaps more important, Goals 2000 lays the conceptual groundwork for other federal legislation, establishing a model for coherence among federal and national endeavors in education that has never been seen before."

• That sounds a lot like what Secretary of Education Richard W. Riley has said, in praising his own ideas and that of the Clinton administration: "When the legislative dust settles and future historians examine the Clinton administration, they will devote a major chapter to the Goals 2000: Educate America Act . . . Like President Lincoln's Morrill Act of 1862 and President Johnson's Elementary and Secondary Education Act of 1965, President Bill Clinton's Goals 2000 Act will stand as an educational beacon."

• And the president himself has said: "Goals 2000 is a new way of doing business in America. It represents the direction our government must take in many problems in the twenty-first century."

Looking at the president's other initiatives — particularly in the area of health care — we should understand precisely what he means. It is Big Government in the service of the new morality, a point of view that argues it's okay to smoke marijuana if you don't inhale. As all of these commentaries have suggested, Goals 2000 is an enormous step in the direction of a nationalized educational system, one that uses federal dollars as bait to hook state and local schools districts and reel them into the boat.

Here are some of the major problems with the Goals 2000 legislation, problems that those who support the program regard as virtues. For starters, Goals 2000 provided for the creation of a National Education

Standards and Improvement Council (NESIC). The purpose of NESIC: to "identify areas in which voluntary national content standards need to be developed." Though the Council has never been appointed, the standards are appearing all over the place, like toadstools after a heavy rain. For example, the National Standards for United States History, produced by the Center for History in the Schools, could well have been written by a consortium composed of members of the National Organization of Women, the Nation of Islam, the National Gay and Lesbian Task Force, and the America Last Committee. So far these standards are voluntary. How long before they're mandatory?

Another provision of Goals 2000, the Opportunity-to-Learn Standards, will mandate that schools who receive federal dollars under Goals 2000 must provide a number of "resources" in order to be eligible. Of this provision, former Assistant Secretary of Education Diane Ravitch has written that "the new standards, euphemistically called 'opportunity-to-learn' standards, would permit Federal regulation of curriculum, textbooks, facilities and instructional methods. . . . The bill describes the Federal opportunity-to-learn standards as 'voluntary,' but litigation would quickly turn them into mandates."

And she's right. Anyone who thinks the school isn't providing enough "gender equity materials" or "minority textbooks" could haul the district or state into court and force compliance with these voluntary standards. Thus this segment of Goals 2000 is an invitation to litigate and will cost school districts millions of dollars in addition to their freedom.

Title III of Goals 2000 authorizes block grants to the states in return for which the federal government requires that a state adhere to federal guidelines for reform, including "opportunity-to-learn standards and curriculum content standards. But even more ominous, this segment of the legislation promotes the transformation of schools into centers where students and parents may receive medical care, counseling, and child care. This kind of "center" bears a striking similarity to a "school-based clinic" — an idea perennially promoted by activists who wish to change the attitudes of young people about such basic matters as sex outside of marriage, homosexuality, contraception, and abortion. In fact, this has been a grand scheme of the Left for decades, a scheme that assumes parents are unable to take care of children, that the family is the chief enemy of social progress in America. Now there is a legislative basis for the development of such clinics or "centers."

These, then, are three of the many irrelevant or destructive programs administered by the U.S. Department of Education. At best these expensive experiments have failed to improve schools that seem to be getting worse by the hour. At worst, they are assaults on the intelligence and decency of American children, outright deterrents to the restoration of right order in our schools. Either way, they are extremely costly.

The Constitution of the United States does not provide for a federal role in education. In fact, the Tenth Amendment clearly implies that schools and learning fall within the purview of the states, which in turn delegates much of that power to the local school districts, who in turn pay a lion's share of the bill. Yet the federal government gets more bang for its buck than either state or local governments because it steps in with enticements tied to policy changes — like an irresponsible uncle who corrupts nieces and nephews with candy and trips to the theater while their parents feed them, clothe them, house them and supply them with the practical necessities of life.

There's only one thing way to handle such a problem: Tell Uncle to butt out. Abolish the U.S. Department of Education and take the first step toward the restoration of order and excellence in our public school system.

5

Support the Human Life Amendment

Most Americans rightly look with suspicion on any move to amend the Constitution of the United States. Some amendments have been necessary and good, but others have caused more problems than they've solved. Still others have responded to specific political or social ills that might have been eliminated in other ways. The Constitution is a sound document and, under ordinary circumstances, should be left alone.

However, these are not ordinary times — not when over a million unborn children are killed every year.

Clearly, something strange and perverse has taken place in our society: Five Supreme Court Justices, none of them elected, have presumed to overturn legal traditions of long-standing and rule that women in America have a right to abort their unborn children. Not only did the High Court in its ruling *allow* the killing of the unborn, but it actually forbade government at any level from passing laws to *prevent* this practice, thereby nullifying laws in a majority of the states.

Avoiding the key question — Is an unborn baby a human being? — Justice Harry Blackmun, in *Roe v. Wade*, argued that women could choose to have an abortion because they enjoyed a "right to privacy." The result of this decision: over 30 million abortions to date, women racked with guilt, and a new cavalier attitude toward life that has led to "mercy killings," assisted suicides, and a first lady who has suggested she doesn't think the elderly should receive lifesaving surgery because it places a strain on the health-care system.

No, these are not ordinary times. The Supreme Court has exceeded its authority, handed down a legally unsound and morally reprehensible decision, and the only way to correct this error is with an amendment to the U.S. Constitution. Never have circumstances more persuasively mandated such an action.

Having made that point, it's important to add that in so amending the Constitution, we would not be contradicting a statement in the original document or even enunciating a new idea. The Declaration of Independence states that all human beings are endowed by their Creator with certain unalienable rights, and that among these are *life*, liberty, and the pursuit of happiness. The framers of the Constitution never dreamed that the country would come to a moment when the Supreme Court would be overruling the laws of the States, much less that the Justices would be saying people had the right to withhold life from a defenseless unborn child. Certainly no right to abortion is currently in our Constitution, nor has it ever been.

So the Unity Human Life Amendment will do more than restore one of those rights specifically enumerated in the Declaration and understood by the founding fathers to be "unalienable." It is only in our bizarre and disoriented times that such an amendment could be called radical. (Ironically, if we lived in normal times, the Court would never have dared to make such a ruling.)

What, then is in the Unity Human Rights Amendment? Here are its major points.

1. Section 1 states that "The right to life is the paramount and most fundamental right of a person." Certainly no reasonable man or woman could quarrel with such a statement.

2. Section 2 makes a crucial clarification of Section 1: saying "With respect to the right to life guaranteed to persons by the fifth and fourteenth articles of amendment to the Constitution, the word 'person' applies to all human beings, irrespective of age, health func-

tion, or condition of dependency, including their unborn offspring at every stage of their biological development including fertilization." This provision assures that not only the unborn, but also the elderly and sick will not, at some future date, be deemed expendable by an even more irresponsible High Court.

3. Section 3 states that "No unborn person shall be deprived of life by any person: *Provided, however,* that nothing in this article shall prohibit a law allowing justification to be shown for only those medical procedures required to prevent the death of either the pregnant woman or her unborn offspring, as long as such law requires every reasonable effort to be made to preserve the life of each." This provision, very carefully phrased and qualified, allows laws to be passed permitting doctors, under restrictive circumstances, to save the lives of mothers and hence is still "pro-life."

4. Section 4 states: "The Congress and the several states shall have power to enforce this article by appropriate legislation." This section merely provides a framework within which to enforce the amendment.

This, then, is the Unity Human Life Amendment. It is a *clarification* of the Constitution with which a majority of Americans can agree, an interpretation that would correct the wrong-headed misreading of the Supreme Court without really altering the nation's most sacred political document. In effect, we would restore the original understanding of the Constitution that in a better time allowed all the states to pass statutes outlawing random abortion. The amendment would merely right a grievous wrong — and nothing more.

To be sure, it would take a great deal of courage for the current Congress to pass such an amendment and send it to the several states. The National Organization for Women, NARAL, and a number of groups favoring abortion on demand would turn up the heat, knowing that their Armageddon was at hand. However, once the amendment passed both houses of Congress with a sufficient margin, then it would probably be approved by three-fourths of the states with far less difficulty. Grassroots America will not oppose a proposition so modest and so reasonable.

Let's ask Congress to pass *this* amendment in *this* form *this* session.

Meanwhile, as the amendment makes its way through a lengthy process of ratification, Congress must turn its attention to the federal government's current role in promoting and funding abortion. Given the deep divisions that exist in the country over this issue and the bitter debate that continues to tear us apart as a people, it is only fitting that federal agencies refrain from sponsoring abortions with the tax dollars of people who believe the practice to be immoral. Prudent legislative and executive branches would at least maintain a neutral stance, neither challenging the decision of the judiciary nor thumbing their nose at the majority of the people who oppose unrestricted abortion. Yet both the Congress of the United States and the president have put their stamp of approval on bills that actually appropriate money for perfectly healthy women to kill their unborn children, in many cases because their pregnancies are merely inconvenient or embarrassing.

In fact, pro-abortion funding has been bootlegged into a number of bills, including Title X, Medicaid, foreign aid, and "project grants" given by the Department of Health and Human Services. In 1993, for example, of the 21 HHS project grants on a list furnished to Congress, Planned Parenthood affiliates received 8 — more than one-third, and several of the rest went to organizations promoting so-called "abortion rights," groups such as Women Organized for Reproductive Choice, the Population Council, and the Center for Population Options.

But the Planned Parenthood grants are particularly significant, since this organization performs more abortions than any other single group in the nation. Here are some of the figures derived from Planned Parenthood's own 1991 "Service Report."

> • A full one-third of Planned Parenthood affiliates — 57 out of 171 — now perform abortions, a proportion that is rising, up from 36 in 1980.
> • In 1991, two more affiliates en-

tered the abortion business, and an additional 16 have resolved to begin performing abortions.

• Combined with the 57 already in the business, that would bring the total to 75, or 44 percent of the total.

• Approximately one in 25 Planned Parenthood "patients" received an abortion in 1990.

Family Research Council offers some additional figures concerning Planned Parenthood:

• In 1993, Planned Parenthood received approximately $37 million from the federal government alone.

• The organization's "haul" from government at every level — federal, state, and local — exceeds $200 million annually.

• Planned Parenthood performs around 125,000 abortions in the United States every year and is involved in promoting over 50 million more worldwide.

• Family Research Council reports that: "The women obtaining divorces from Planned Parenthood have been disproportionately poor and members of minority groups."

It is important to realize that one of Margaret

Sanger's original purposes in founding an organization addressing questions of birth control was to reduce the number of minorities in America, with the idea of breeding a more racially homogenous people. As she herself said, she wanted to create "a race of thoroughbreds" — an effort described by supporters as *eugenist*. Later, in her autobiography, she put it this way: "The eugenists wanted to shift the birth control emphasis from less children for the poor to more children for the rich."

"Stop the multiplication of the unfit" is a euphemism worthy of a Mengele. Abortion certainly fits that description, as — from the perspective of a Nazi — so did the ovens at Auschwitz. With World War II already begun and theories of a "master race" in disgrace, Sanger changed the name of her organization to "Planned Parenthood." But the aims and tactics have been the same, as the statistics on minority abortions suggest.

By the way, in a single year, 1993, the U.S. Department of Health and Human Services gave Planned Parenthood and its affiliates a total of over $8 million in discretionary grants. How much of that money went to abortions would, of course, be a matter of dispute. It's difficult to pinpoint the impact of such an influx of cash on the activities of an organization. Planned Parenthood of Wisconsin, Inc., for example, received two grants in that year, the first for $270,184, the second for $2,542,125. How much of that went to abortion-related activities?

Of course, the Clinton administration — which has pushed for abortion quietly while the president says publicly that he wants to reduce the number — now allows Planned Parenthood to "co-locate" abortion clinics and family planning clinics. Such a ruling will surely encourage more Planned Parenthood affiliates to get into the game.

And speaking of the president, in 1993 he issued an executive order that lifted the ban on abortions in the military. This order, sent directly to the Pentagon, said simply: "I hereby direct that you reverse the ban immediately."

As noted by Col. Robert Maginnis of Family Research Council, the immediate result of this order: nothing happened. Heroic military doctors refused to perform the abortions voluntarily, and women who wanted to kill their unborn children had to go to foreign doctors. It was a remarkable exercise of moral principle on the part of medical personnel in our armed forces — and an illustration of the invasion of conscience that occurs when government promotes the killing of the unborn.

Later, however, doctors were dispatched to Germany who were willing to perform abortions. The president seems determined to push the this unconscionable practice where he has the authority to do so unilaterally — for example, when acting as commander in chief of the armed forces.

And then there's Medicaid.

For 17 years, the Hyde Amendment banned the use of federal funds for Medicaid abortions except in cases where the life of the mother was threatened. This restriction was reasonable, given the strong feelings of millions of Americans — indeed, according to every public opinion poll, a substantial majority. Liberals as well as conservatives routinely voted for the Hyde Amendment since they knew a majority of their constituency approved of it.

Then the Clinton administration came to power and a Democratic majority in both houses of Congress altered the Amendment's wording, "broadening" the language to include rape and incest. The current Hyde Amendment sounds the same to the general public, yet opens the door to widespread misuse, since "rape" can be a highly subjective word. The result: a policy that has allowed more women and their doctors to elect abortions paid for by Medicaid — i.e., by the nation's taxpayers.

Again, a majority of Americans who supported the original Hyde Amendment were told that a portion of their taxes would be used to routinely fund procedures they believed to be morally wrong except to save human life. Such reckless courting of animosity from the nation's voters involves either a degree of ideological zealotry or else an abject fear in the face of women's pressure groups. And it's difficult to conclude that at least some of the defeats that Democrats suffered during the 1994 electoral rout were the result of this slackening of the national resolve to prevent abortion on demand.

The Hyde Amendment in its original form should be reintroduced at the earliest possible moment, if it has not already been passed by the time this book is published. Such sensible, mainstream legislation has been missing during the first two years of the Clinton Administration. It should be revived and extended into other areas of federal funding. In summary, we need a "Hyde *Act*" that would unequivocally ban any federal funding of abortion except in cases where a woman's life is genuinely in danger and any promotion of abortion, either domestically or abroad.

As for the funding of abortion in the international community, the foreign aid program involves billions of dollars shipped abroad with the active encouragement of the American government to use part of the money for "population control," another euphemism for killing unborn children. In fact, the Clinton Administration sent an infamous telegram to the U.S. diplomatic corps, instructing them to push for more abortions in every country where an embassy or consulate was located — **even in nations where the practice was illegal**. Thus were our overseas diplomats instantly transformed into active ambassadors for Planned Parenthood.

As I said in the Introduction, sometimes politics is the art of the impossible. It is perhaps unlikely that a Unity Human Life Amendment to the U.S. Constitution can be passed during this session. The Democratic Party is committed to the agenda of the radical feminists, and the Republican Party has a number of pro-abortion members in its midst.

In addition, the president of the United States has seemed more and more determined to promote federally funded abortion, despite the fact that then-Governor Clinton said as recently as September 26,

1986: "I am opposed to abortion and to government funding of abortions. We should not spend state funds on abortions because so many people believe abortion is wrong."

But despite the odds against us, we must not give up on this issue or put it "on the back burner." Lives are at stake, and the soul of the nation hangs in the balance. We cannot survive for long, torn apart as we are. If we persevere — if we make our case clearly and eloquently to the American people — there is a chance that we may be the beneficiaries of a great miracle, the kind that can only be brought about through the intervention of the Holy Spirit in the lives and hearts of millions of Americans. He wants to bestow this kind of grace. But we have to be willing to receive it. And willingness implies a belief in miracles.

6

Pass a School Prayer Amendment

In 1962, after almost 200 years of stable government, the Supreme Court ruled that it was unconstitutional for children to say prayers in school. Many people believed the decision was no more than a fine point of law — nothing that would substantively affect the way in which children grew up or adults led their daily lives.

In the three decades that have followed, America has changed radically. Indeed, the alterations in the nation's moral and spiritual life have been greater in the past 30 years than in the first 180. In 1986, David

Barton, in his thoughtful book *America: To Pray or Not to Pray,* catalogued these changes and argued that the Supreme Court's 1962 decision was the single event that triggered a sudden and precipitous decline in the character of the nation. His case is well-documented and statistically credible. It must be taken seriously.

Below are a few of Barton's significant findings, as well as a number of additional figures gathered from government sources. These statistics, particularly those relevant to the sexual conduct of our young people, constitute the *Mene Mene* on the walls of America's schools.

• The academic achievement of American students has plunged over the past three decades. The year in which this rapid decline began: 1962.

— In 1962, average SAT scores hit their high-water mark of 980.

— By 1972 they had dropped below 940.

— By 1980, they had dropped to 890.

— This decline is not explainable in terms of reduced expenditures. As a matter of fact, according to Dr. Peter Uhlenberg of the University of North Carolina, "in constant 1980 dollars, expenditures per pupil went from $1,248 in 1960 to $2,491 in 1980, a whopping 99.6 percent."

• **The sexual morals of American students began to deteriorate rapidly — after 1962. The figure for girls 15-19 is particularly instructive.**

— In 1960, only 10 percent of teenage girls had experienced premarital intercourse.

— By 1971, the figure had reached 31.7 percent.

— By 1979, it had jumped to 43.4 percent

— By 1988, it had reached 52.6 percent.

• **The sexual activity of adolescent males also increased dramatically during this same period.**

— In 1960, only 25 percent of teenage boys had experienced sexual intercourse.

— By 1979, the figure had reached 65.7 percent.

— By 1988, the figure had risen to 75.5 percent.

• **The same trends have been recorded for women in college.**

— In 1963, 75 percent of the women on college campuses had never engaged in sexual intercourse.

— By 1984, that figure had

dropped to 43 percent.

• College men have also exhibited the same pattern in sexual conduct since 1962.

— In 1963, 40 percent of college males had not yet engaged in sexual intercourse.

— By 1978, the figure had been reduced to 34 percent.

— By 1984, it had further declined to 28 percent.

• Pregnancy rates among adolescent girls (age 15-19) rose alarmingly from 1962 to 1988.

— These rates in 1962 were 99 pregnancies per 1,000.

— In 1980, they had increased to 111 per 1,000.

— During the 1980's, when the Reagan administration began to stress abstinence and family values, the rates leveled off. But they have never returned to the 1962 level.

— Over the past seven years, over a million adolescent girls have become pregnant every year.

• There are no reliable figures for abortion rates in 1962, since abor-

tion was illegal in most states. In 1973, after *Roe v. Wade*, it was possible to keep national records. Predictably, abortion rates have climbed since that time.

— In 1974, 29 percent of adolescent pregnancies ended in abortion.

— By 1980, the figure had risen to 41 percent, where it stabilized. For example, in 1985, 42 percent of adolescent pregnancies were terminated by abortion.

— Younger adolescents are more likely to terminate a pregnancy by abortion than are older adolescents, with 56 percent of pregnancies terminated by abortion among girls under 15.

• Out-of wedlock births among adolescents have increased over the years, despite the enormous rise in numbers of abortions.

— In 1970, 29.5 percent of births to adolescents were out-of-wedlock.

— By 1988, the figure had risen to 65.3 percent.

— In 1988, 91.2 percent of births to black teens aged 15-19 were out-of-wedlock.

— In the same year, 53.3 percent of births to white teens were out-of-wedlock.

— Between 1970 and 1988, out-of-wedlock births for white adolescents increased at a rate of 213 percent, while the increase for blacks was 45 percent.

While it is impossible to prove that the banning of school prayer was the direct and only cause of this moral decay, there is clearly a connection. Perhaps the fact that a climate existed within which the High Court could make such a decision is explanation enough for the onset of a documentable rise, not only of those problems listed above, but also in drug use, violence, and crime among our young people. Whatever the reason, the American people have consistently favored the reinstatement of prayer — and by overwhelming numbers. As a matter of fact, for the past three decades support for prayer in schools has remained at around 70 percent. There are very few subjects on which the public is more likely to agree.

One of the most remarkable characteristics of Americans is their continued adherence to religious principles in large numbers. A majority of Americans continue to go to religious observances despite the decline in traditional morality. Such is not the case in other Western nations. Almost no one goes to church in Great Britain. Attendance in Catholic France, Spain, and Italy has fallen off over the past four or five decades. And this decline in faith has continued despite the fact that European schools offer religious instruction while it has been forbidden in American classrooms.

It is difficult to explain this phenomenal survival of faith in the United States, but there is no guarantee that it will last forever — not with the active repression of religion by the federal government, which increases year by year as the courts extend the boundaries of the prayer decision.

- Children have been forbidden to mention the word "Christmas" in many schools throughout the nation, and manger scenes have been banished from public squares. The celebration of such religious occasions as Christmas and Easter, which long ago took on a cultural significance that transcends mere sectarianism, have been ruthlessly purged from public life; and their disappearance may have a profound effect on the psyche of the nation.

- Despite its literary, cultural, and historical significance, the Bible has been banished from the public schools. A teacher in one school was ordered to remove his own personal Bible from his desk, despite the fact that he never read aloud from it to his students.

- A student group that wished to assemble in an empty classroom for Bible study after school was told they could not do so. (They later appealed the decision in the federal courts and won.)

• It is perhaps relevant to note at this point that the U.S. Department of Health and Human Services reports that "adolescents who say that religion is important to them are less likely to be sexually active than those who say it is not very important." This fact establishes a direct correlation between the sexual conduct of young people and the absence of religious faith in our schools. It is ironic that our federal and state governments are willing to do anything, however vulgar and offensive, to prevent teenagers from becoming pregnant or diseased, but they are forbidden by law to rely on the one resource that seems to work.

As noted elsewhere, the High Court's decision to ban prayer in public schools was largely the result of one woman's assault on the traditional understanding of the relationship between church and state. For the better part of two hundred years, a consensus existed on what the First Amendment meant and what it did *not* mean, particularly in relation to the so-called "establishment clause," which was originally and properly understood as a prohibition against the federal government establishing a national church and funding it with tax dollars.

This amendment was passed for good historical reasons. A number of the first settlers on these shores had fled England in order to escape the oppression of religious "dissenters" by the Church of England, which was established and supported by the state and interwoven into the very fabric of public life. The founders wished to make certain that such a national church never dominated the spiritual life of citizens of the United States.

On the other hand, several of the states already had instituted "established" churches prior to the time of the Constitutional Convention. Massachusetts, for example, had designated the Congregational Church as the "state church," and all taxpayers contributed to its support, whether they attended or not. So the First Amendment was not adopted in order to eliminate state churches; indeed, it could be argued that the establishment clause was attached to the First Amendment in order to *protect* the right of the states to "establish" churches.

In fact, Thomas Jefferson — always cited as the most "free thinking" of our founders and a man who opposed the creation and funding of state churches — nonetheless, in his Second Inaugural Address, specifically stated that the states had the right to "prescribe religious exercises."

> In matters of religion, I have considered that its free exercise is placed by the constitution independent of the powers of the general (federal) government. I have therefore undertaken, on no occasion, to prescribe the religious exercises

suited to it; but have left them, as the constitution found them, under the direction and discipline of state or church authorities acknowledged by the several religious societies.

This statement deserves careful reexamination, and for several reasons:

- Unlike his oft-quoted remark concerning "the wall of separation," this firm declaration was not a vague metaphorical expression of personal opinion made in a private letter but a precise and deliberative phrase spoken as president of the United States at a formal state occasion.

- Jefferson says here that while the president does not have the right to prescribe religious exercises (i.e., prayers and other religious observances), the states clearly *do* have that right under the Constitution.

- But he goes further: He even states *why* the states have such rights: because they brought them into the Union when they ratified the Constitution. Thus a state's right to prescribe religious exercises *preceded the Constitution itself.*

In making such a statement, Jefferson was not

merely expressing a private opinion. His argument against the establishment of a church in the state of Virginia prevailed; and unlike Massachusetts, the Old Dominion State did not make the Episcopal church, or any other denomination, the official state church. But however much Jefferson may have disapproved of the idea, when he made his report to the nation at the end of his first term, he felt obliged to remind the American people that (1) the federal government can't establish religious practices and that (2) the states can.

Yet in 1962, the Supreme Court overruled the founding fathers, overruled Thomas Jefferson, and overruled the practice of almost two centuries by declaring prayer in schools unconstitutional. It was an arbitrary imposition of personal will by five men who shared Jefferson's view that the states should not establish religious exercises and failed to match his integrity in recognizing that they had the right to do so.

Granted, we have come a long way from the founding and the states rights position of Thomas Jefferson. Certainly no one — not even the leadership of the religious right — would propose that states be allowed to establish churches or even that sectarian prayers be prescribed in our classrooms. However, to prohibit prayers in public schools, in public buildings, and at public occasions constitutes a violation of the First Amendment and has the effect of driving religion from the communal life of the American people. In addition, that 1962 ruling has led to the "establishment" of radical secularism as the "religion" of the U.S. government — a secularism as oppressive as the European regimes of another era. The governmental attacks on religion documented elsewhere in this volume must be stopped.

We must therefore pass an amendment to the U.S. Constitution that would clarify the meaning of the "establishment" clause and allow non-sectarian prayers in our schools. If such an amendment is not passed, we will have forfeited our religious freedoms and the traditional commitment to faith that has made the United States of America a great and good nation.

7

Reinstate the Ban

     The prohibition against homosexuals serving in the U.S. armed forces has been a sound policy, one based on strategic considerations rather than bigotry. The current policy — commonly described as "don't ask, don't tell" — compromises our military and as a consequence poses a potential threat to the nation's survival, if not today then at some time in the future. The ban on homosexuals in our armed forces must therefore be reinstated, and for the very same reasons it was instituted in the first place.

     In 1981, these reasons were spelled out in Department of Defense Directive 1332.14 as follows:

     The presence in the military environment of persons who engage in homosexual conduct or who, by their statements, demonstrate a propensity to engage in homosexual conduct, seriously impairs the accomplishment of the military mission. The presence of such members adversely affects the ability of the military services (1) to maintain discipline, good-order, and morale; (2) to foster mutual trust and confidence among service members; to insure the integrity of the system of rank and command; (4) to facilitate assignment and worldwide deployment of service members who frequent must live and work under close conditions affording minimal privacy; (5) to recruit and retain members of the military services; and (7) to prevent breaches of security.

This list of reasons may make more sense to people with military experience than to those who have never served, so perhaps they need some clarification.

> *To maintain discipline, good order, and morale; to foster mutual trust and confidence among service members.*

Introducing a sexual element into basic training, barracks or ship life, and combat missions would further complicate conditions that are already, at times, strained. Most young men and women who enter military services are not used to living in close quarters with members of the same sex, undergoing rigorous training, and at some point even risking their lives together in combat. Since homosexual men are known to be much more active sexually than heterosexual men, incidents will inevitably occur that will undermine the closely knit camaraderie that holds a military unit together. In such situations, irreparable damage may be done to the discipline and effectiveness of our fighting forces. Colonel David Hackworth, writing in the *Washington Post* (June 28, 1992), and Kevin McCrane, writing in the *Wall Street Journal* (December 2, 1992), tell of incidents that occurred in an earlier era, when homosexuals were still banned from the armed forces.

> • Hackworth tells of a soldier who "could not keep his hands off other soldiers in my squad." The result: the homosexual "mangled trust among squad members and zeroed out morale."
> • He also recalls "a gay commanding officer gave combat awards to his lovers who had never been on the line."
> • McCrane, a businessman rather than a career member of the military, tells of sexual harassment on shipboard, when he was a young sailor in 1945: "It was in the open now, a subject for discussion, among the new recruits. Each of us had

been accosted, patted, and propositioned. Though we were in different divisions, we flocked together for meals, averting our eyes when one of "them" leered in our direction. There were five such aggressive homosexuals that we knew of aboard this ship with almost 20 men. They were all petty officers. Their actions were enough to poison the atmosphere on the *Warrick*. Meals, showers, attendance at the movies, decisions about where you went on the ship alone — all became part of a worried calculation of risk."

It is well to remember that these breaches of discipline, good order, and morale occurred at a time when homosexuals were forbidden by law to serve in the military. Clearly such incidents will multiply in a service that allows homosexual enlistment and winks at their behavior, saying, "As long as you don't get caught, you can behave as you please."

To insure the integrity of the system of rank and command.

Chain of command is essential to any military operation, from conducting basic training to a dangerous engagement with the enemy. Subordinates must obey those in command without questioning motive or integrity. Any breakdown in discipline can be disastrous, even fatal to a combat unit. That's why the sexual orientation of officers and NCO's must be above suspicion. Under the new policy, enlisted personnel may be subject to sexual harassment and promise of reward from superiors who seek their favors. Colonel Hackworth again speaks to the subject.

> • He tells of a captain in Vietnam who was propositioned by his commanding officer and says the incident "almost destroyed the esprit of a fine parachute unit."
>
> • He cites the case of a homosexual personnel major who "had affairs with ambitious teenage soldiers in exchange for kicking up their test scores."
>
> • In summary, Colonel Hackworth observes: "These are not isolated incidents; during my army career I saw countless officers and NCO's who couldn't stop themselves from hitting on soldiers. The absoluteness of their authority, the lack of privacy, enforced intimacy, and a 24-hour-duty day made sexual urges difficult to control."

To facilitate assignment and worldwide deployment of service members who frequently must live and work under close conditions affording minimal privacy.

Colonel William Woodruff, a published authority in the field, writes in *Family Policy:* "Bathing and sleeping facilities traditionally have been segregated by gender because the vast majority of men and women are attracted to the opposite sex and view being forced to sleep, shower, and use toilet facilities with members of the opposite sex as an infringement of privacy. When individuals of the same gender find members of the same gender sexually attractive, the same invasion of privacy occurs even in gender-segregated facilities." His logic is beyond refute.

In addition, there are many countries in the world where homosexuality is looked upon as a grave transgression of the law. Members of the American armed forces stationed in such countries would encounter additional problems if homosexuals were allowed to serve legally. Under the old policy, few such complications arose.

To recruit and retain members of the military services.

Polls show that current members of the military have consistently opposed admitting homosexuals to the armed forces, whether openly gay or content to remain in the closet. Many of these are likely to leave military service if the present policy is allowed to stand. Also, many young people contemplating a career in the military service will be repelled at the thought of having to live and work closely with people who are attracted to others of the same sex.

At present, no one knows the impact of the current policy on retention and recruitment, and such an impact may not ultimately be measurable. But the information already gathered suggests a high level of dissatisfaction among current service members. Should the present policy generate more friction between homosexuals and heterosexuals — which seems likely, given the reduced risk for homosexuals — the level may rise even higher.

To maintain public acceptability of military service.

Historically, Americans have been proud of their armed forces; and that justifiable pride has led them to support the military in the field. During the Vietnam War, when support among civilians markedly declined, the effect on the morale of those serving was obvious. Fortunately, the sense of pride returned with Operation Desert Storm and subsequent actions in Somalia and Haiti. So the relationship between the American people and their armed forces is crucial to the continued survival of both.

The civilian population, though tolerant of aberrant behavior, disapproves of homosexuality and does not wish to see such a "lifestyle" given official sanction by the U.S. government. Likewise, knowing that the armed forces are now open to gays, civilians are likely to view service members from a slightly different perspective — with less respect, more suspicion, and even contempt. Such a change in attitude can only result in a less content and less effective military.

To prevent breaches of security.

Despite the fact that Secretary of Defense Dick Cheney called this objection "a bit of an old chestnut," we have learned following the collapse of the Soviet Union that Russian spies routinely targeted gays for special scrutiny, since they knew homosexuals were more likely than heterosexuals to have problems with alcohol and drugs.

In addition to the reasons outlined in this directive, there are other justifications to exclude homosexuals from the armed forces. Perhaps the most important of these is the medical problems that homosexuals bring to military service. These have been well-documented in *Exclusion: Homosexuals and the Right to Serve,* an authoritative study by Major Melissa Wells-Petry, published in 1993. Among other things, she shows that homosexuals are far more sexually promiscuous than heterosexuals. Here are a just a few of the studies she cites, all from leading medical journals.

- A study of intravenous drug users concluded that "homosexual men . . . reported a median of 1,160 lifetime sexual partners, compared with . . . 40 male heterosexual intravenous drug users."
- Another study reported that "homosexual men had significantly more sexual partners in the preceding one

month, six months, and lifetime (median 2, 9, and 200 partners, respectively), than the heterosexual subjects (1, 1, and 14 partners)."

• Still another study revealed that while "the median number of lifetime sexual partners of the [more than] 400 [homosexual] respondents was 49.5. Many reported ranges of 300-400, and 272 individuals reported 'over 1,000' different lifetime partners."

Needless to say, such promiscuous conduct among homosexuals inevitably leads to a much higher incidence of sexually transmitted diseases and other contagious afflictions spread through intimate contact.

• One study reported that 65.5 percent of the sample had contracted gonorrhea, 52.5 percent had contracted hepatitis, 40.8 percent had contracted genital warts, and 36.7 percent had contracted syphilis.

• Another study revealed that "in addition to high rates of gonorrhea, syphilis, and hepatitis B, gay men have shown to be at high risk for venereal transmission of anorectal venereal warts, hepatitis A, enteric pathogens, and cytomegalovirus infections."

• Yet another study revealed that

homosexual men are "predisposed to acquiring organisms that are sexually transmitted during rectal intercourse."

• And there are other risks involved in these practices. One hospital conducted a study of trauma resulting from anal intercourse. Among other facts, the study reported: "A series of 101 patients with trauma of the rectum, secondary to homosexual practices, presenting at this hospital is reviewed. Two patients were injured twice. Thirty-six patients had retained foreign bodies in the rectum, 55 had lacerations of the mucosa, two had disruptions of the anal sphincter, and ten had perforations of the rectosigmoid."

• Studies show that "82 percent of homosexual patients and 72 percent of homosexual control subjects reported [practicing anal intercourse] . . . and cancer risk for men who expressed a homosexual preference [was] more than 12 times that for heterosexual men."

It is important to remember that many recruits entering the military service for the first time are still in their teens. In 1990 the American Medical Association, in a key study on adolescent health, cited a report that concluded that homosexual adolescents were 23 times more likely than heterosexual adolescents to contract a sexually transmitted disease.

The summaries of medical studies, however unpleasant to read, indicate the difficulties our military hospitals will encounter if the number of homosexuals in the military continues to increase as the result of current policy. Such crises on permanent bases will overburden a medical staff prepared to deal only with the usual diseases and injuries. In the field — and particularly in combat situations — the additional demand for medical services from gay personnel could result in confusion, frustration, and loss of life. Imagine the difficulties of the M*A*S*H unit had they been forced to deal with some of the diseases and traumas mentioned above, even as the wounded were arriving by helicopter.

Finally, it's important to understand that the civil rights arguments gay rights activists offer to justify a lifting of the ban do not apply in this case. For one thing, military service cannot be compared to the general workplace. The courts have routinely upheld the right of the military to "discriminate" against a number of groups, on the very good grounds that only those experienced in running military operations can know what is best for the various branches of the armed forces.

Melissa Wells-Petry points out that the military have excluded the following from service: the physically handicapped, women in combat units, religious groups (e.g., the Sikhs, who are required to wear their traditional headgear), people who weigh too much or too little, people who are too tall or too short, people who are near-sighted and far-sighted, those who can't speak the English language, and those who haven't graduated from high school.

The reason the courts have traditionally allowed this latitude is because the branches of the armed forces have a unique mission to fulfill in society — that of ensuring the survival of the United States of America. In time of war, when the nation's enemies are threatening to destroy our government and our people, the full efficiency of our military is more important than any other single consideration. Anyone mature at the beginning of World War II understands that unique mission, which the American people supported virtually without dissent.

Today no powerful potential enemies loom on the horizon. For a moment in history, we are the most powerful nation in the world. However, such preeminence may not last more than a few years, particularly if we forfeit our military strength and through neglect allow a diminishing of our capacity to defend ourselves. We've been lax before. We mustn't allow our military to be jeopardized just because we've entered a period of social experimentation and upheaval. Our armed forces are traditional in structure, not merely because they are conservative by nature, but also because, from the beginning of the nation's history, the old rules and prohibitions have worked. Now that we've become the most powerful nation in the world, we mustn't forget how we gained such a position — by observing traditional moral teachings and by keeping our most important institutions free from corrupting influence. In the past two years we've strayed from the path of tradition and honor. We must return to our traditional roots and reinstate the ban on gays in the military.

8

De-fund the Gay Rights Movement

First, we must make a distinction between "homosexuals" and the "Gay Rights movement." The two are by no means synonymous, though gay activists would have us believe so. Homosexuals are people who, for some mysterious reason, are physically attracted to others of the same sex. Despite all the medical propaganda manufactured in the past two or three years, there is no consensus as to why some people develop in this manner. Whatever the reasons, they deserve our sympathy and our prayers.

The Gay Rights movement, on the other hand, is

composed of a handful of homosexuals who promote a political agenda that demands recognition of their behavior as "normal," "natural," and "equal to heterosexuality." They intend to achieve this status by political means — by filing lawsuits in state and federal courts, by passing local and state ordinances giving them special protection in housing, jobs, fringe benefits, and other areas of community life. And eventually they hope to force the Congress of the United States to pass special legislation granting them the same privileges under federal law. Meanwhile, they are well-represented in the Clinton administration and are making enormous progress with a minimum of publicity.

At present, virtually every agency in the executive branch of the federal government is actively promoting the "gay rights" agenda, either through internal "educational" programs or direct funding to homosexual organizations and support groups.

One of the ways in which Congress and the Clinton administration channel federal dollars to the Gay Rights movement is through the enormous amount of money now allotted to AIDS. Here are just some of the homosexual organizations that have received funding for "AIDS education" over the past two years from one program in one agency. In most cases, these groups are using tax dollars not only to talk about so-called "safe sex" as a means of avoiding AIDS, but are also producing homo-erotic materials and gay rights propaganda. While many of the other organizations on the list actively support the same goals (e.g., the San Francisco AIDS Foundation), this list contains only groups whose names identify them as "gay": the National Gay Health Education Foundation, National Association of Black and White Men Together, Los Angeles Gay and Lesbian Community Service Center, Gay and Lesbian Adolescent Social Services, National Latino Lesbian and Gay Organization, National Gay and Lesbian Health Foundation, National Gay Health Foundation, and The Gay Men's Health Crisis.

The majority of the American people are unaware that a portion of their income is being diverted to projects such as these. Most would be appalled at the very idea. It's disturbing enough for government to confiscate a portion of every worker's paycheck and hand it over to people who have lived all their lives on welfare and have no prospect or intention of finding employment. It's infinitely worse to transfer income from America's families to homosexual activists so they can print and distribute propaganda, lobby politicians at every level, and seek special privileges for those who practice deviant sex.

Despite an enormously successful public relations campaign, the Gay Rights movement has been unable to forge a new American consensus on the issue of homosexuality. To be sure, some people have been won over to the cause of gay rights by the well-publicized studies that partisan scientists have manufactured and presented to the general public. Three fairly recent projects — those by LeVay, Pillard, and Hamer — have been offered as "proof" that homosexuality is hereditary.

Despite the fact that all three of these researchers

are homosexual activists whose methodology and objectivity have been called into question by highly reputable authorities in the field, the media have often presented their findings as authoritative and even definitive.

Despite these erroneous accounts, most Americans still reject the idea that homosexuality is "natural" or "normal" and regard such behavior as either a pathology or an example of poor character. In this respect, they are not alone.

Dr. Richard Isay is one of the leading gay rights activists in the American Psychiatric Association and has chaired the American Psychiatric Association's Committee on Gay, Lesbian and Bisexual Issues. I'm sure he would like to persuade every psychiatrist on the planet that homosexuality is normal and natural. Yet he has stated in print that "There is, nevertheless, continuing conviction among most, though not all, dynamically oriented psychiatrists in general and psychoanalysts in particular that homosexuality can and should be changed to heterosexuality by a 'neutral' therapy that uncovers repressed childhood conflict that interferes with 'normal' heterosexual development." In other words, Dr. Isay is admitting that a substantial proportion of such psychiatrists and therapists believe there is something wrong with homosexuals, that they are abnormal and are in need of treatment.

In addition to agreeing with this assessment, many Americans would also say that homosexual behavior is contrary to the laws of God and nature and hence immoral. These opinions grow out of deeply held religious convictions and can be justified by the scriptures of the world's great religions. It is therefore a violation of the First Amendment to use the tax dollars of such people to promote projects and publications that specifically attack their religious beliefs on this issue.

Consider just two examples, funded by taxpayers and published by the United States government:

The Report of the Secretary's Task Force on Youth Suicide

The Secretary's Task Force on Youth Suicide was a product of the Reagan administration and created under the auspices of Otis Bowen, then Secretary of Health and Human Services. Contained in the report of this task force was an essay by Paul Gibson, a "therapist and program consultant" in San Francisco. This essay, entitled "Gay Male and Lesbian Suicide," was a plea for the promotion of homosexuality among the young and an attack on families and specific orthodox Christian denominations.

Of orthodox Christianity he writes:

> Religion presents another risk factor in gay youth suicide because of the depiction of homosexuality as a sin and the reliance of families on the church for understanding homosexuality. Many traditionalists (e.g., Catholicism) and fundamentalist (e.g., Baptist) faiths still portray homosexuality as morally wrong or

evil. Family religious beliefs can be a primary reason for forcing children to leave home if a homosexual orientation is seen as incompatible with church teachings. These beliefs can also create unresolvable internal conflicts for gay youth who adhere to their faith but believe they will not change their sexual orientation. They may feel wicked and condemned to hell and attempt suicide in despair of ever obtaining redemption.

So much for Jefferson's "wall of separation." The government is here attacking specific churches. As Dr. Paul Cameron of the Family Research Institute has written: "If the state is forbidden to promote religion, then it should also be forbidden to attack religion — and especially specific denominations. To identify religion as a 'risk factor' is itself an outrageous tactic for a government-sponsored publication, but to single out two specific communions for special blame seems deliberately provocative, particularly when they are the largest Christian denominations in the country."[2]

In his segment, Gibson is not content to attack specific denomination, but he also calls for sweeping changes in society, the family, and the Church.

To contemporary society he says:

Gay males and lesbians need to be accepted as equal partners in our society. Laws should safeguard their individual rights and not permit discrimination against them in housing, employment, and other areas. Laws prohibiting homosexual relationships between consenting adults should be repealed and marriages between homosexuals should be recognized. Special attention should be paid to the enforcement of laws that punish those who commit violence against homosexuals. Laws can help establish the principle of equality for lesbians and gay men and define the conduct of others in their interactions with them.

We must promote a positive image of gay males and lesbians to reduce oppression against them and provide gay youth with role models to pattern themselves after. Massive education efforts need to take place that would provide people with accurate information about homosexuality. These efforts especially need to be directed to those who have responsibility for the care of the young including families, clergy, teachers, and helping professionals.

To parents he gives the following advice:

Parents should know that homosexuality is a natural and healthy form of sexual expression. They do not need to feel bad about something that is good. . . . Families need to take responsibility for presenting homosexuality in a positive context to their children.

To churches and synagogues he says the following:

> Religions need to reassess homosexuality in a positive context within their belief systems. They need to accept gay youth and make a place for them in the church and include them in the same activities as other youth. Religions should also take responsibility for providing their families and membership with positive information about homosexuality that discourages the oppression of lesbians and gay men. Faiths that condemn homosexuality should recognize how they contribute to the rejection of gay youth by their families and suicide among lesbians and gay male youth.

AIDS, Sexual Behavior, and Intravenous Drug Use

This volume, published by the prestigious National Research Council (NRC), wanders boldly and easily into the thicket of political controversy, using quasi-scientific mumbo-jumbo to criticize religion for its role in "stigmatizing" homosexuality:

> In this epidemic the rationale rests

on the fact that AIDS is transmitted by seemingly voluntary behaviors that are widely disapproved of in the broader society. In the vocabulary of some religions, these behaviors are called "sinful." Accusers can say to victims, "If you hadn't behaved in this or that shameful or sinful way, this wouldn't have happened to you." This direct attribution of responsibility feeds one of the essential features of stigmatization: blameworthiness. It allows society to feel justified in excluding victims from concern or banishing them from the community. One group that is especially prone to stigmatization is gay men.

But the volume goes even further, suggesting that the orthodox religious view of homosexuality (and also of drug addiction) is in reality a "pathology" — that is, a mental illness.

The deeply rooted *social pathology* [emphasis added] of stigmatization is not easy to dispel. Even when revealed for what it is, the psychological and social mechanisms that support stigmatization may resist eradication. Rational appeals to understanding are necessary and sometimes useful, but they are often frustrated by forces deeper than reason.

Then, in one of the most outrageous violations of the First Amendment in recent memory, a volume funded by the federal government tells Christian clergy precisely what they should say about homosexuality in the pulpit.

> Churches, whose involvement in stigma has historically been great — both as objects and agents — can preach an enlightened view and demand of their adherents sympathy and justice.

Cameron's commentary is apt: "Surely this is unprecedented from an agency of the federal government — an order to Christian preachers to demand a particular social attitude from their congregations. The word 'demand is singularly harsh and suggests how ignorant the committee is of the relationship between most clergy and their 'adherents.'"

At this point, it's important to note that Christians and social conservatives have often been accused of trying to impose their moral views on other people. Such is certainly not the case in this controversial area. No responsible spokesman for the Right has proposed legislation proclaiming that homosexuality is immoral, nor has anyone argued in favor of a federal law outlawing sodomy. We are perfectly content to let the states and local governments handle such matters as they choose.

Nor is anyone suggesting agencies of the federal government should promote approval of Christianity or biblical morality among all workers. We have not urged the organization of Christian employees in the various departments, nor have we decreed that those who wish raises or promotions should join religious organizations outside the workplace or become members of Christian activist groups.

On the other hand, homosexual activists have done all of the above — and with the blessing of the executive branch and without serious objection from the U.S. Congress.

• Almost every agency in the executive branch has promoted "diversity in the workplace," which has paid lip service to respect among various racial and ethnic groups but is really aimed at lecturing those who disapprove of homosexuality. These programs have made the point that homosexuality is "normal," "natural," and therefore "good" — just as former Surgeon General Joycelyn Elders said. It's as if the federal government were telling those employees who were orthodox Jews and Christians that they had no right to believe what their synagogues and churches taught them.

• In addition, almost every agency now has a gay employees organization, which is actively working to promote gay issues within government. These organizations are not merely tolerated but encouraged by the agency heads and by the Clinton administration.

• At least one federal agency — the Department of Housing and Urban Development — has told its senior employees that if they wish to be considered for raises or promotions, they must be active in some outside service or political organization. One suggested activity — participation in a gay or lesbian activist group.

So who is attempting to impose their values on government in particular and the American people in general? It's not the social conservatives, the radical right, or the evangelical fringe. It's the homosexuals and they are succeeding — with the help of the executive branch and the Congress of the United States, which has been pouring money into gay rights causes since the Carter administration.

One of the most outrageous appropriations of federal funds by gay rights advocates occurred in the National Cancer Institute (NCI). Despite the fact that federal funding for AIDS research has reached the point where it now surpasses funding for cancer research and heart research, a homosexual scientist, Dean Hamer, managed to commandeer NCI funds and set up a project to determine whether or not homosexuality was influenced by genes. An entire laboratory at the National Cancer Institute was devoted to this study, which was clearly designed to prove a genetic link to homosexuality that would reinforce the Gay Rights movement's push for special treatment under the law.

Hamer's research was rushed into print in *Science,* a magazine that in recent years has devoted more and more space to gay rights issues and taken an active role in promoting the theory that homosexuality is normal and deserving of special legal protection. The networks in turn interviewed Hamer, who, according to reliable reports, agreed to appear only if his own homosexuality was concealed. Well-established experts in the field of genetics have challenged both the methodology and significance of the Hamer study, but the media have repeatedly cited the work as "part of the growing body of evidence" that homosexuality is inherited, like skin color and gender.

In the meantime, more people die in one year from cancer than have died in the entire history of the AIDS epidemic, which many see as subsiding. Clearly the victims of cancer and their loved ones have not organized themselves as well as have the homosexuals, who fund political candidates, stage demonstrations featuring strident placards, disrupt public meetings, and launch elaborate publicity campaigns to make certain their disease receives preferential treatment by government at every level. Thus AIDS activists have succeeded in diverting tax dollars to their malady at the expense of cancer victims and heart patients.

And tragically, some of this funding supports politically motivated research and propaganda in the form of "AIDS education." Thus the state of Minnesota has received money from the Centers for Disease Control to publish a pamphlet justifying homosexual behavior to young people. Indeed, some pro-family researchers have argued that gay rights literature disguised as AIDS education is a chief purveyor of the movement's message, that without federal funding of this nature, the Gay Rights movement would soon wither away and die.

Again, we do not ask that federal legislation be passed outlawing sodomy. (The situation in our armed forces poses special problems that do not exist in society at large.) We do not ask that religious attitudes toward homosexual behavior be affirmed by federal agencies. We do not ask that homosexuals be barred from government service. We do not ask that federal employees who are homosexual be barred from organizing themselves.

We do ask that no federal legislation be passed affirming homosexuality, particularly in view of the fact that the Supreme Court has ruled that state anti-sodomy laws are constitutional. We do ask that the federal government cease its funding of anti-religious materials, particularly as they relate to this issue. We also ask that federal agencies be forbidden by law from presenting pro-homosexual programs and materials to agency employees. We do ask that homosexuals who wish to organize be instructed to do so on their own time and off the premises of government buildings and property, just as religious people must now do.

We also ask that the government cease the funding of printed materials that in any way promote the idea that homosexuality is normal, natural, healthy, an acceptable lifestyle, a product of genetic factors, or the idea that those who believe homosexuality is immoral, unhealthy, or a bad habit are ignorant or bigoted or unworthy of serious consideration. In point of fact, all of these questions are the subject of continuing debate, both in the religious community and in the scientific community. The government has no right to intervene in behalf of a homosexual community that continues to spread a variety of diseases and in the process costs the American taxpayer billions of dollars.

The inclusion of sexual orientation in the hate-crimes bill was the first acknowledgment by the Congress of the United States that it regarded the status of homosexuals as somehow comparable with that of blacks and other ethnic minorities. This recognition, however well-intentioned, was a major concession to gay rights forces and an incentive for homosexuals to seek further legislation that would grant them special rights under federal law. This law should be amended to remove sexual orientation from the specific categories included under hate crimes statistics. Such action should be taken in order to reaffirm the neutrality of the federal government in the current debate over homosexuality in American society. Homosexuals, after all, are protected from all crimes just as heterosexuals are. There is no reason for the U.S. Government to adopt a policy that seems to grant special protections against crime to those who engage in deviant sex.

Currently the Gay Rights movement, either directly or indirectly, is receiving millions, perhaps billions of dollars annually from the federal treasury —

and at a time when the federal deficit is approaching 4 trillion dollars. A Congress that appeases this small but virulent minority by appropriating huge sums of money for its benefit can never be trusted to balance the budget or to practice fiscal responsibility in any other area of government. While the de-funding of the Gay Rights movement may not solve the problem of a deficit increasing by hundreds of billions every year, it is a necessary beginning, an exercise in the kind of courage necessary to solve the large problem.

9

Abolish the Endowments of Hatred

The National Endowment for the Arts and the National Endowment for the Humanities are among the most cherished of government's sacred cows — two frivolous and troubling agencies whose continued existence mocks the idea that Congress seriously intends to reduce the deficit. Though they have many problems in common, each of the Endowments has its own history of controversy, so they must be examined separately.

The National Endowment for the Arts

Prior to the 1980s, the National Endowment for the Arts was a little-known federal agency administering a modest budget. Today the NEA is a topic of conversation among millions of Americans who never go to art museums or symphony concerts, much less to a performance by Holly Hughes or Karen Finley. The agency has attracted this attention because it funds obscenity and religious bigotry and then thumbs its nose at the taxpayers who foot the bill. In fact, its fame was spread worldwide during the 1995 Academy Award ceremony, when performer after performer — beginning with Academy President Arthur Hiller — put in a plug for the NEA. For years now Hollywood performers have come to Washington and appeared before congressional committees in support of continued government funding for the arts. They give the usual arguments: that art plays a constructive role in society, that many local activities such as symphonies and art associations are supported by federal dollars, that a number of European governments support painting and music and filmmaking, and that the NEA costs so little that the average taxpayer is assessed no more than a few pennies a year.

Let's consider these arguments one at a time before listing the very good reasons why the NEA should be abolished.

1. Arts plays a constructive role in society.

Often it does. But art can be destructive as well,

since anything powerful enough to move people to do good can also move them to do evil. To suggest otherwise is to say that novels and paintings and films are finally irrelevant. A careful examination of Nazi and Soviet art will illustrate this point.

So art is not necessarily a constructive force in society. But even if that proposition were true, you couldn't automatically conclude that the government should be funding the arts. People can agree that religion plays a constructive role in society and still not insist that the government should fund churches and synagogues. There are many essential segments of our society that the government doesn't support. These other activities compete in the market place, as the arts did until a few years ago, when Senator Pell proposed that government should begin to fund art as the icing on the huge cake that government presents annually to the American people. Unfortunately, some of what the NEA has funded is the kind of art that contributes to the disintegration of society rather than its cohesiveness.

2. Many local activities such as symphonies and art associations are supported by federal dollars.

True enough. However, you must keep two things in mind.

First, these activities thrived long before the National Endowment for the Arts was established and will continue to do so long after it has been abolished. For decades, independent home-town symphonies, "little theaters," and local art festivals have borne witness to the enormous fertility of creative America. Such activities don't need artificial insemination by a Washington bureaucracy.

Second, while it's true that the NEA funds some worthy productions, the deliberately offensive projects cannot be justified. If the Endowment were sponsoring a handful of racist or anti-Semitic artists, its current apologists would immediately understand that no list of praiseworthy grants, however long, could excuse such an unconscionable misuse of tax dollars. They must therefore realize that millions of Americans feel the same way about a homosexual orgy or a photograph depicting a crucifix suspended in urine. Though such works constitute a minority of projects funded, their outrageous nature more than counterbalances the more wholesome activities supported by the NEA.

3. A number of European governments support painting and music and filmmaking.

Yes, they do. And virtually all of them also offer religious education in state-supported schools, as well as a number of other "services" that Americans believe are inappropriate for government to undertake. Many of these nations are more socialized than we are. (Communist nations were quite generous in funding the arts.) Most European governments exert far greater control over their citizens. For example, they often require the carrying of identification papers. And by the way, in most Western nations citizens have a much easier time suing reporters and editors for libel, which is why the

British media are more careful about what they print; but that's not an argument for doing things the same way in this country. Which country do we admire so greatly that we would adopt all of its laws and customs, while scrapping our own? Let's not worry about what other nations do.

4. The NEA costs so little that the average tax-payer is assessed no more than a few pennies annually.

Again, the argument is irrelevant. One penny assessed for hate literature is one penny too many. The problem lies not in the amount but in the principle. American taxpayers should not be compelled to fund projects and artists they regard as incompetent, taste-less, or perversive — not even to the tune of a single penny.

These, then, are the major arguments offered in favor of the National Endowment for the Arts. They rest mostly on sentimental or highly questionable assumptions — that artists are somehow a downtrodden lot in need of a hot meal and new shoes, that the arts will wither and die without massive federal funding, that artists somehow have the right to offend those who pay their water and light bills. Clearly such assertions are without merit in an age where Jasper Johns gets proportionally more for his paintings of American flags and herringbone patterns than any artist in the history of the world, including Michelangelo, Rembrandt, and Picasso.

And there are compelling reasons why the federal government should *not* fund the arts, some of which have nothing to do with whether or not some people are offended by the works of Andres Seranno or Robert Mapplethorpe. Here are just a few of those reasons.

1. The federal government shouldn't fund the arts for the same reason it shouldn't fund a national church — because to do so is to "establish" (that is, to give official sanction to) ideas and tastes that are fiercely held and highly personal.

In other words, people are just as entitled to their tastes in art as they are to their religious beliefs; and it's wrong for a handful of people to decide that the federal government should fund one church over another, or one type of art over another. This argument cannot be dismissed merely because the First Amendment forbids the establishment of a national church and not a National Endowment for the Arts. We don't oppose the establishment of a national church merely because it's contrary to the First Amendment. We do so because it's a bad idea. And it's a bad idea because it would run roughshod over deeply-held individual convictions. If the arts are important at all, then individual aesthetic convictions deserve the same kind of respect as religious convictions. And if the arts aren't important, then we ought not to be funding them in the first place.

2. The NEA has "politicized" the arts in every sense of the word and in so doing cheapened and

corrupted the creative process.

In the first place, from the very beginning the Endowment itself has been a nest of political intrigue. Various factions in the art world initially vied with one another to control the board, the staff, and the panels that awarded grants. For example, from the advent of the first Director, the gay influence has been pervasive. Holly Hughes, Mapplethorpe, and many, many other artists have received funding for projects with aggressively homosexual subjects and themes. People are not offended by the fact that these artists are homosexual but rather that the works they have produced are flamboyantly and sometimes obscenely gay. The defiance they exhibit in continuing to produce "shock-art" is born of the knowledge that they have control of the grant-making process and are therefore safe from reprisal.

On the other hand, other groups — for example, representational painters — have no chance to win grants because the process is under the control of critics and fellow artists who look with contempt on their kind of art. If you are a portrait painter whose faces and flesh tones look like real human beings, then in all likelihood you're out of luck. Your enemies have captured all the panels. A drawing class was turned down for a grant because the teachers were subjecting the students to a traditional discipline. The panel in rejecting the application called the approach "fascist." So one faction has political control of the Endowment, and its members distribute tax dollars to one another as if they'd earned the money themselves.

The NEA is also politicized in a broader sense. Its subject matter is increasingly political and frequently partisan. Thus "Sex Is. . . ." — a film depicting homosexual acts and funded by the NEA — contains a mock dedication "to the memory of Jesse Helms" and an ironic recitation of the restrictions the senator proposed, restrictions that the film itself proudly, defiantly violates, with its explicit scenes of anal and oral sex.

Thus the NEA grants money to its friends who in turn use the funding to attack the Endowment's critics. When political art is funded (which it frequently is), it is invariably the art of the Left, with its slashing attacks on conventional morality, law and order, fiscal conservatism, and religious orthodoxy. In fact, one of the most disturbing aspects of NEA grants under the past three administrations is its general anti-Christian bias and its specific focus on the Roman Catholic church and on evangelical Protestants. Political satire has existed in every age, and no one is suggesting that it should be censored. On the other hand, should government itself be partisan and ideological in its funding of such satire? Or, to put the question in simpler terms: Should government be funding political art at all, or does its participation call into question the integrity of such works?

4. Given the current level of the national deficit, we can no longer afford to fund the arts.

Let's look for a moment at the plight of a real middle-class family facing a financial crisis. The father, the chief wage earner, is a college professor. He and his wife appreciate nice things, but his income is insufficient to afford expensive works of art. However, by saving and sacrificing, they bought a Picasso lithograph, one of the great artist's many doves. It was signed in pencil and one of 50 numbered prints. They were lucky to pick it up for $5,000 from a small art dealer.

They've owned the picture for two years, but this year they have run into unexpected financial difficulties, and suddenly they have incurred debts they are unable to pay. The interest on their loans and credit cards is eating them alive, and they see no increased income to cover the indebtedness. They take a look at their budget and their holdings to see what can be done. One thing is certain: They have a picture hanging on their wall that can help them reduce their indebtedness and find a little breathing room. They hate to see it go, but they come to an inevitable conclusion: With all the other bills to pay, they can't afford to keep the Picasso — which is a luxury. They sell the picture for $7,500, pay off some of their debts, and see the monthly outflow reduced. They can stop eating canned food bought at the salvage store and buy new clothes for the children in the fall.

The situation described here (a true story) is not identical with that of the federal government, but some of the same principles apply. The federal deficit is a cause for deep concern among experts in both political parties. Clearly Congress and the White House must make major cuts in spending if this growing problem is to be solved. Yet our leaders apparently lack the courage to reduce government sufficiently to balance the budget.

While the Endowments are only a small item, their symbolic value in the fight against the deficit is enormous. They have been in existence only a short time. They involve the government in activities not authorized under the Constitution. In short, they constitute a luxury — small but not irrelevant to the big financial picture. If you add up the amount spent on the NEA, the NEH, PBS, NPR, and a host of other marginal items, the figure climbs into the low billions. And as Everett Dirksen said, "A billion here, a billion there — pretty soon you're talking about real money."

5. Millions of people are appalled by the subject matter of the art funded, which they regard as obscene and a deliberate affront to their moral and social values.

It is this objection to the NEA that receives the most attention, though it isn't necessarily the most important. Still, you have to wonder at the logic of a system that says that people must be forced to pay for art that deliberately sets out to mock them and offend their sensibilities. Nothing of the sort has happened before — certainly not in the greatest periods of artistic achievement.

Apologists for the NEA are constantly pointing to historical precedent for state funding of the arts in the great rulers of cities, states, and kingdoms who have generously supported the greatest artists of all time. And to be sure, the history of art is full of such arrangements. However, no great patron of the arts ever funded works he or she considered unappealing, obscene, or contrary to deeply held beliefs.

- Vergil, seeking a grant from Augustus Caesar, devoted a segment of his *Aenead* to the praising Augustus's family. Had he attacked either Caesar's ancestors or his reign, he would have been cut off without a drachma.
- Does anyone really believe that the Pope would have paid Michelangelo had the great artist painted a picture of Christ suspended in urine on the ceiling of the Sistine Chapel? Had he presumed to do so, Michelangelo would not only have been de-funded, but might well have been boiled in oil.
- Francis I would never have permitted Benvenuto Cellini to create a piece of sculpture that attacked the king's policies and politics — not while Cellini was on the king's payroll.

During the period when artists worked for great princes or great prelates, they created the kinds of works that pleased their patrons; and when they failed to do so, they were quickly de-funded. In theory these artists were limited by the taste and intellect of their patrons. In practice, some of the world's greatest art was created under such a system.

In the later eighteenth century and early nineteenth century, with the advent of Romanticism, artists began to chafe under the mild yoke of court patronage. They had come to see art as "self-expression" rather than the imitation of nature or the creation of beauty. And given such a belief, they no longer wished to accept the conditions of the patron in exchange for his gold. So they moved into garrets, wrote and painted and composed for themselves — and starved. It was a fair bargain: In exchange for absolute freedom, the artist was willing to forego his place at the center of society and the financial security that went with such a role.

Now, in the latter half of the twentieth century, artists want to have it both ways: They want the American people to serve as their patrons and yet have the same absolute license enjoyed by the artist in the garret. It can't work that way. The American people's tax dollars cannot be handed over to any agency or individual with no strings attached. That's precisely what went wrong with the S&L's. We removed restrictions on these institutions while guaranteeing the accounts of depositors against disastrous speculation. Likewise, we take money in the form of taxes from wage earners, then give it to artists who are free to insult and affront their benefactors. In both cases, the American people are justifiably outraged.

Yet the artists have a point. They can't allow Joe Six-Pack to tell them what they can and can't do on a canvas or in a poem or with a camera. Art doesn't work that way, particularly in the twentieth century.

Likewise, it would be impossible for Congress or the NEA or any other body of regulators to establish specific guidelines that would satisfy both the American people and those seeking grants. Language is inadequate to resolve all potential problems and reconcile all conflicting opinions in this large and highly fragmented society. There is no common ground on which opposing sides of this debate could stand. Therefore, the only solution is to cease federal funding of the arts and admit that in a pluralistic society — one that can no longer depend on a consensus for deciding what is moral or aesthetically pleasing — a National Endowment for the Arts is a practical impossibility.

If you are one of those people who doesn't really know what the National Endowment for the Arts has done to stir up such fierce controversy, then consider the following examples in which NEA (i.e., taxpayers') dollars have been involved.

• Andres Serrano received support to produce a photograph of a crucifix suspended in urine. The title of the work: "Piss Christ."
• Funded by the NEA, Robert Mapplethorpe produced a series of photographs which included graphic homosexual scenes: one man urinating in another's mouth, the artist parading naked with a bullwhip inserted in his rectum, and anal intercourse.

• At a theater funded by the NEA, "Father Larry" — a performer dressed as a priest — closed his act by charging into the audience, tearing the clothes off two young men, and sodomizing them.

• Annie Sprinkle, performing naked at another theater receiving NEA support, inserted a bottle in her vagina, then invited the audience to give her a gynecological examination with a flashlight. She boasted onstage that her act was courtesy of the National Endowment for the Arts.

• Holly Hughes, an avowed lesbian, also performed naked in an act that featured obscene invective. She, too, received an NEA grant.

• Karen Finley, whose feminist diatribes featured obscene language and acts, including a naked skit in which she rubbed chocolate all over her as a symbol of excrement.

• *Tongues of Fire,* a film about homosexual Black men, was screened nationally by PBS and seen during prime time in major markets nationwide, though some stations refused to carry the broadcast. In addition to explicit shots of homosexual acts, it featured ponderous and pretentious doggerel that sounded as if it had been written by a group of self-preoccupied high school seniors.

• Gay and lesbian film festivals in San Francisco have received annual funding, despite widespread protests from outraged individuals and pro-family groups.

• In 1993, through a regional grant the Endowment funded "Sex Is. . . ." a film that depicted explicit shots of homosexuals masturbating, performing oral sex, and engaging in group sex. In addition, one segment was devoted to a man dripping hot candle wax on another while engaging in anal sex. Far from being a skillfully wrought production, the film was badly photographed, badly lit, and badly recorded. In quality as well as subject matter, it resembled hard-core pornography. Now out on videotape, it is too amateurish and foul to be carried in Blockbuster stores.

These projects are only the more obvious examples of the objectionable materials funded by the National Endowment for the Arts. Many other works were also obscene, also devoid of artistic merit, also offensive to large segments of the population — including millions of taxpayers.

In the final analysis, the Congress of the United States is responsible for the perpetuation of this perennial assault on the dignity and good taste of the American people. The willingness of its Members to continue funding of the NEA in the year 1995 would not constitute proof of their commitment to support of the arts. To the contrary, it would be evidence that they are little more than a congregation of yahoos — devoid of aesthetic judgment, devoid of critical principles, devoid of a commitment to genuine craftsmanship and good taste.

The National Endowment for the Humanities.

As for the National Endowment for the Humanities, most Americans probably don't know it exists, much less what it does. By federal standards, it's a small agency with a tiny budget. However, in terms of the academic marketplace, its impact is substantial. While research grants for scientists are relatively easy to come by, funding for the humanities — literature, languages, history, the social sciences — is sparse and usually comes from a limited number of foundations. Therefore, as far as colleges and universities are concerned, the NEH, with its "relatively small" budget, is the last of the big spenders.

And what kind of projects does the agency fund? Are they as offensive as those funded by the National Endowment for the Arts or is the NEH a benign and even friendly force abroad in the nation? Sheldon Hackney, the politically correct head of the National Endowment for the Humanities, recent told a House subcommittee that his agency was so bland and non-controversial that he was beginning to worry. As he put it: "We haven't done anything that has outraged any significant group lately. We wonder if we are becoming appropriately adventurous." Two sentiments in this short sentence suggest serious problems with the NEH.

First, his use of the word "significant" implies that as long as you don't offend one of the larger, more powerful organizations in the country, you need not worry about the rest of the people. If you just offend Grandma — or, for that matter, a million unorganized grandmas — you're entitled to boast before the Congress of the United States.

Second, the statement implies that unless you *are* offending significant groups, you may not be "adventurous" enough. In other words, the purpose of the NEH is to "push the envelope," to promote studies that will offend somebody, anybody — as if the only kinds of projects worth funding are those that affront society. That's a good leftist position, one that makes the humanities no more than an instrument for radical social reform. It fails to recognize the obvious truth that there are probably an infinite number of possible projects the agency could fund that might enrich the humanities without offending a single soul on the planet earth.

Besides, the real reason large quantities of people aren't offended by recent NEH grants is because they don't know what's been going on. Peter Warren, writing in the March 28, 1995, *Washington Times*, pointed out that last spring's awards focused on what Warren calls "the holy trinity of race class and gender issues." He cites as examples four grants given to Duke University for projects that were ideological in concept:

- "Berisso Obero: Class, Gender, Ethnicity and Construction of Identity in an Argentine Labor Community"
- "The Comintern and South Africa"
- "Cherokee Removal and American Resettlement of Cherokee Lands"
- "Exile and Crisis of Cultural Identity in Contemporary Hispanic Literature."

Warren's comment on these and other examples he cites is worth preserving: "There is nothing intrinsically wrong with studying issues of race, class, and gender. But the NEH's unremitting support of Marxist and Foucaultian approaches to the subject grows tiresome." Indeed, it does. With Marxism in shambles worldwide — its model empire gone, its principal politicians in disgrace — Americans must find it ironic that their government persists in promoting this discredited approach to the problems of our age. The fact that the NEH continues in this vein, indicates the bankruptcy of the American intellectual establishment and the ideological narrowness of Sheldon Hackney and his cohorts. If this is the kind of research being conducted in our universities, we don't want to nurture it with federal dollars. We want to starve it to death, so that something a little more creative and innovative can come into being.

Yet it would be a mistake to believe that should the Republicans win the White House in 1996, things would necessarily change. There has always been a certain amount of mutual back-scratching in the NEH, regardless of who controls the agency. The truth is, American academics are fighting a fierce, no-holds-barred ideological war with one another, and the greatest casualties (aside from the students) are genuine ideas. This is the very worst of times to pour tax dollars into academic research. The Endowment will inevitably be politicized in approximately the same way that the universities are. Thus we will continue to waste money in an effort to offend the American people when colleges and universities are fully capable of giving offense without any government support whatsoever. Why pay for something when you can get it for nothing?

Even more to the point, remember that it was the National Endowment for the Humanities, along with the Department of Education, that funded the infamous "history standards." These standards — what every American student should know about American history — were released to the world at an opportune time, just after the Republicans captured the Congress. Thus were the newly elected members able to see the potential danger in the agency — a danger that only a handful of Washington observers had previously appreciated.

Among other outrages, these NEH-sponsored standards (funded when George Bush was in the White House and Lynne Cheney was heading the NEH):

> • emphasized a multi-cultural approach that focused on minority figures

and cultures while neglecting major episodes in American history,

> • omitted any mention of Robert E. Lee but referred to the Ku Klux Klan 17 times, and

> • talked about "Soviet advances in space" but neglected to cite the fact that the United States had landed astronauts on the moon.

This agency is a drain on the budget and a drag on the imagination. It should be offered to the Ford Foundation and the Rockefeller Foundation for five cents on the dollar.

In fact, both the NEH and the NEA are at best luxuries in a time of financial crisis, at worst reminders that something is gravely wrong in the nation's artistic and intellectual communities and that many of our writers, scholars, and performers are actively attempting to destroy the traditional institutions of American society. If members of Congress continue to vote financial support for this activity, they and the American people will be accomplices in their own undoing.

10

Abolish the Office of Surgeon General

Once upon a time, the surgeon general of the United States was the head of the Public Health Service and actually directed its activities nationwide. To understand precisely how the office worked, let's take the example of Dr. Thomas Parran, who was surgeon general under Roosevelt and Truman. He took office during the Great Depression and served through World War II — times that placed an additional burden on all public servants. But he was not famous for his work on malnutrition or the wounded, but rather for his campaign against a disease whose name he could not even speak on national radio. Thomas Parran was the surgeon general who almost eliminated syphilis in the United States.

He realized that the disease could be all but wiped out if certain standard medical procedures were followed, including widespread testing and contact tracing. Though Parran lived at a time when federal authorities had very little to do with disease, he initiated testing in a number of federal agencies and also managed to use the power of his office to promote testing and contact tracing in the private sector.

- He instituted testing in the WPA, the CCC, the TVA, and other government-funded projects.
- When the draft was re-instituted in anticipation of World War II, he tested every man who reported for a physical — virtually the entire male population between the ages of 17 and 40. Eventually Selective Service medics administered tests for syphilis to over 25 million citizens.
- He persuaded steel manufacturers and other heavy industries to initiate testing among their employees, starting at the top.
- He persuaded the state of Alabama to test every citizen between the ages of 15 and 55, and the U.S. Public Health Service furnished the supplies

and medical personnel to do the testing.

By the middle 1940s, syphilis was almost eradicated in the United States, largely because of Parran's ability to marshall his Public Health Service in what became an all-out war on the disease. Many people regard Parran's pro-active style as another example of improper involvement by the federal government in matters constitutionally delegated to the states. However, one thing is certain: His comprehensive campaign against syphilis was government intervention at its best.

Contrast Parran's remarkable record with the failure of three successive surgeon generals to address the AIDS epidemic in a traditional and effective way. C. Everett Koop, Antonia Novello, and Joycelyn Elders — far from showing courage in the face of a loud and unruly group of militant homosexuals — all advocated a retreat from proven strategies for dealing with sexually transmitted diseases, though Novello was less vocal than the other two.

Koop's *Surgeon General's Report* was perhaps the most influential public document on the subject. Published in 1986 — just when public opinion on AIDS was crystallizing — it propagated misinformation and promoted dangerous health practices. Among other things, Dr. Koop wrote in his report:

> Some personal measures are adequate to safely protect yourself and others from infection by the AIDS virus and

its complications. Among these are:

> If your test is positive or if you engage in high risk activities and choose not to have a test, you should tell your sexual partner. If you jointly decide to have sex, you must protect your partner by always using a rubber (condom) during (start to finish) sexual intercourse (vagina or rectum).
>
> If your partner has a positive blood test showing that he/she has been infected with the AIDS virus or you suspect he/she has been exposed by previous heterosexual or homosexual behavior or use of intravenous drugs with shared needles and syringes, a rubber (condom) should always be used during (start to finish) sexual intercourse (vagina or rectum).

Note what the surgeon general of the United States said here, in an official government report at the beginning of a killer epidemic: (1) if you are infected with the HIV virus or your sexual partner is infected, all you have to do to "safely protect yourself" is to use a condom; and (2) that this advice is just as sound for vaginal intercourse as for anal intercourse. It was precisely what the homosexual community wanted to hear: the orgy could continue; all they had to do was use condoms.

But Koop had no scientific evidence to support this statement. As a matter of fact, there was plenty of evidence that condoms were highly fallible, even for the prevention of pregnancy. The failure rate — published independent researchers such as the Consumer's Union — consistently hit about 10 percent for all women, and about 16 percent for younger women, who were much more fertile (i.e., teenagers). Since the AIDS virus was tiny compared to a sperm, many researchers were skeptical about Koop's optimistic assessment.

- Dr. Margaret Fischl, conducting research at the University of Miami, reported in 1987 on 18 married couples who used condoms during intercourse because the husband was infected with AIDS. In an 18-month period, despite the condoms, three of the wives became HIV-positive.

- Dr. James Goedert of the National Cancer Institute, wrote of condom use when one partner was infected: "there is no acceptable level for this risk. 'Lower risk' is an inadequate goal and perhaps even a vacuous notion" (*The New England Journal of Medicine,* May 1, 1987).

- Dr. Harold Jaffee, chief of epidemiology at the Centers for Disease Control , was quoted (*New York Times,* August 18, 1987) as follows: "You just can't tell people it's all right to do whatever you want so long as you wear a condom. It's just too dangerous a disease to say that."

Suddenly the surgeon general was on the defensive. Koop began to back and fill as quickly as he could.

• In the September 18, 1987 issue of *USA Today* Koop said, in replying to a question about the reliability of condoms in preventing AIDS: "The country has become involved in 'condom mania.' I don't feel particularly happy about the role I've played in that. Condoms are a last resort. I have never failed to go through a litany that the only way you can avoid AIDS is through abstinence." (There was no such litany in his report.)

• In the same interview, when asked "Are condoms a valid protection in anal intercourse?" Koop said: "The rectum was not made for intercourse. It's at the wrong angle. It's the wrong size. It doesn't have the same kind of tough lining that the vagina does. It has its blood supply directly under the mucosa. Therefore you would expect a great many more failures of condoms in rectal intercourse than you would in vaginal intercourse, and it's important to know that."

(Note, he makes no such distinction in his report.)

• In an editorial for the *Journal of the American Medical Association* (October 16, 1987), Dr. Koop wrote: "Do not practice anal intercourse; the rectal mucosa bleeds easily and provides an entry for HIV. Condoms provide some protection, but anal intercourse is simply too dangerous a practice. Since the AIDS epidemic began, the majority of AIDS cases in the United States probably became infected by anal intercourse." (But anyone who read his report — and there were millions distributed — would have come to an entirely different conclusion.)

• In an interview at UCLA (September 22, 1987), Koop took back virtually everything, according to the *Los Angeles Times,* saying "that prophylactics have 'an extraordinarily high' failure rate among homosexuals and offer them no assurance of 'safe sex.' " (But his report is still being quoted today as the ultimate authority on this subject.)

Whether Dr. Koop simply made a monstrous error in judgment or whether he listened too carefully to homosexual activists, eager to sustain their movement, his cavalier advice probably cost lives — and only the good Lord knows how many. Instead of following

Parran's example and pushing for testing and contact tracing, he viewed the issue not as a doctor but as a civil libertarian — and with his loud opposition to standard medical practice, the chances to contain the epidemic went down the tube. The homosexuals blame Ronald Reagan for the AIDS quilt. Perhaps they're partially right. He did, after all, appoint C. Everett Koop.

Perhaps the single most persuasive argument in favor of abolishing the office of surgeon general is Joycelyn Elders — the most recent holder of that title. Appointed by President Clinton, Dr. Elders came to Washington bringing with her a reputation for outspoken advocacy of explicit sex education, condoms for adolescents, and easy access to abortion. She was known in Arkansas as a woman fanatically dedicated to reducing the unwanted pregnancy. Yet during her tenure as head of the state's Department of Health, the pregnancy rate rose 15 percent. This rise was attributable in part to the fact that she and other Arkansas educators ignored the most objective and comprehensive government studies on teenage sexual behavior, which showed that programs stressing birth control and condoms do not reduce teenage pregnancy, but that several well-known abstinence-based programs are effective.

Despite her failure to accomplish her goals in Arkansas, President Clinton appointed her surgeon general of the United States, where she again began to speak out in favor of sexual license, abortion, and even legalization of drugs. Indeed, her statements were so outrageous that the president eventually had to ask for her resignation. Among the more memorable are the following:

> • In supporting sex education, she was quoted by the West Memphis, Arkansas *Evening Times* (March 4, 1992) as saying: We taught them what to do in the front seat [of a car]. Now it's time to teach them what to do in the back seat."

> • As surgeon general, she said that the federal government has the responsibility to teach homosexual youths how to use condoms. (*The Advocate*, March 22, 1994).

> • In an interview with the *New York Times*, she said: "If I could be the 'condom queen' and get every young person who is engaged in sex to use a condom in the United States, I would wear a crown on my head with a condom on it."

> • Elders was a vocal proponent of federally funded abortion, even when she was still in Arkansas. *National Review* (April 26, 1993) quotes her statement that "if Medicaid does not pay for abortions, does not pay for family planning, but pays for pre-natal care and delivery, that's saying: 'I'll pay for you to have another good, healthy slave. But I won't pay for you to use your brain and make choices for yourself. . . .' It's a way

to keep people poor, ignorant and en-slaved. If you are poor and ignorant, you are a slave."

• At a January 1992 "Rally for Reproductive Freedom" in Little Rock, Elders claimed that abortion held down the number of unwanted children brought into the world and estimated that 57 per-cent of children were unplanned and un-wanted.

• On August 14, 1993, she was quoted by the *Washington Times* as say-ing: "Abortion has an important and posi-tive public health effect.

• She called Christians who op-pose abortion "very religious non-Chris-tians" who "love little babies as long as they are in someone else's uterus. She specifically attacked the Roman Catho-lic Church for its stance on abortion, contemptuously calling it a "celibate male-dominated church."

• Elders was a strong supporter of gay rights and homosexuality. President Clinton had said during the 1992 cam-paign that he believed that, as a private organization, the Boy Scouts of America should be able to exclude homosexuals. However, in *USA Weekend* (June 3-5, 1994), Elders said in an interview:

Q: Did you say you believe the Boy Scouts should admit homosexuals?

A: Yes. I also think girls who are lesbians should be allowed to join the Girl Scouts.

• As surgeon general, Elders parroted gay rights propaganda in proclaiming the homosexual behavior as "normal" and "healthy." In an interview with the homosexual magazine *The Advocate* (March 22, 1994), she was quoted as saying: "Society wants to keep all sexuality in the closet. We have to be more open about sex, and we need to speak out to tell people sex is good, sex is wonderful. It's a normal part and healthy part of our being, whether it is homosexual or heterosexual."

• Though AIDS is only number nine on the list of killer diseases, it now receives more funding than either the number one killer (heart disease) or the number two killer (cancer). Elders apparently saw nothing wrong with this discrepancy and gave her reason why: "Most of the people who die with heart disease and cancer are our elderly population...we all will probably die of something sooner or later." (Quoted in the *Washington Post*, June 23, 1994)

• Elders said on more than one occasion that she favored the legalization of drugs. On December 8, 1993, the *Washington Post* quoted her as saying: "... we would markedly reduce our crime rate if drugs were legalized."

• On another occasion, she went even further, favoring government dispensing of drugs to addicts: "When we say 'legalize,' I'm really talking about control. We [could] have doctors or clinics set up where addicts could get their drugs free or pay one dollar."

• So sympathetic was she to drug use that she even thought of those women who supported their habit through prostitution: "I would hope that we would provide them with Norplant, so they could still use sex if they must to buy their drugs" (*Washington Times*, June 23, 1994).

It is easy enough to say that Joycelyn Elders was no more than an aberration, a poor choice for an essential position. But it has become increasingly obvious that the surgeon general has little more to do than speak out on health issues and that a shock-jock approach is already something of a tradition. To be sure, Antonia Novello, George Bush's surgeon general, was a low-key figure, and a marked contrast both to her predecessor and her successor, but she too made statements supportive of the Gay Rights movement and failed to use her office, as Parran did, to promote standard medical practices in dealing with AIDS.

No one seems to do a very good job in this office. Let's abolish it and live happier and healthier lives.

11

Spending Money on a Free Press?

Nothing is more frustrating to millions of Americans than the idea that their tax dollars are being used to fund obscenity, anti-religious bigotry, and anti-American diatribes. Yet when they turn their radio dial to National Public Radio (NPR) or the Public Broadcasting System (PBS) this kind of programming is exactly what they hear and see. And when they call or write to protest, they are told — usually in very polite and circumlocutious language — to mind their own business.

Yet most of these people have the very distinct

idea that "public" radio and "public" television *are* their business, and that they should have some say-so about the nature of the programs that are broadcast. Indeed, the more they think about it, the more they question the very existence of a Corporation for Public Broadcasting (CPB), which is the organization that sponsors public radio and public television. Here are two questions that immediately come to mind.

Question # 1. Shouldn't Congress or somebody be exercising greater control over the Corporation for Public Broadcasting and its television and radio operations?

Back in the good old days, when a radio performer told an off-color joke or used a four-letter word, the program immediately went off the air and the audience heard recorded music for the remainder of the time allotted. Somewhere in the bowels of the network, a censor had earned his money by throwing a switch to protect the sensibilities of children and decent adults. The network provided the censor.

Times have changed, and the networks now seem more concerned with ratings and with topping the competition by airing programs that shock decent Americans. Even sponsors seem reasonably immune to public protest, though the American Family Association has done much to educate major corporations concerning their responsibility to the pro-family community. Still, the networks *are* privately owned. Public broadcasting, on the other hand, is funded by tax dollars, and for that reason is subject to congressional oversight. So why isn't Congress doing its job?

Other government agencies must submit to strict oversight by congressional committees and subcommittees. During the long reign of Democrats on Capitol Hill (40 years with a majority in the House), oversight committees were forever poking their noses into the activities of the State Department, the Justice Department, the Defense Department, and the Department of Education. Chairmen of committees and subcommittees could call hearings, demand information, and cross examine executives almost any time of the day or night. And when they didn't like what was going on, they changed the law the next time an authorization bill came up for a vote.

Indeed, when the Republicans held the White House, it seemed as if Democrats spent all their waking hours scrutinizing the executive branch in order to protect the American people from bad public policy. Fair enough. The bureaucrats who run federal agencies aren't elected. Members of Congress are. They act in behalf of 248,000,000 Americans, most of whom don't live in Washington and don't know the first thing about how the government is supposed to operate. We all believe in checks and balances. Shouldn't they also operate in the cases of agencies like CPB, PBS, and NPR — particularly because they have upset so many people? And if there hasn't been close oversight by Congress and a correction of offensive policies and programming, then why not? If you get government money, the oversight and control come along with it.

That's the way Uncle Sugar operates. Ask anyone receiving farm subsidies or buying a house on a GI loan. As a matter of fact, when the government gives or promises money without strict regulation, trouble inevitably follows. Perhaps the most dramatic recent example is the failure of several major S&L's because the industry was deregulated while the government was still guaranteeing losses with tax dollars. In the world of finance, that's called "a scandal." In the world of news and entertainment, it's called "artistic freedom." But whatever it's called, it's unrealistic and irresponsible.

Note the dilemma of the national press in dealing with the issue of the Corporation for Public Broadcasting. On the one hand, for years PBS and NPR have been sending out a politically correct message to its viewers and listeners, the same message that the major newspapers and television networks are disseminating. So the press has every reason to support Public Radio and Public Television as allies in the political and cultural wars.

On the other hand, the press has constantly prided itself on its distance from government, its objectivity — achieved in part by the wall of separation the press believes it has erected between itself and those who serve in government. We constantly hear stories of reporters who have refused the favors and intimacies of the White House or Capitol Hill because they didn't want to compromise their objectivity. Yet here are news reporters whose salaries are paid by the taxpayers and who must submit to some oversight by the Congress and the president, since either has the power to wipe out the agency with a stroke of a pen.

Most of the working press does not worry about this dilemma. They are happy enough to depict the current cry for the abolition of CPB as nothing more than a bunch of yahoos opposed to the "Three Tenors" and "Sesame Street." But a perceptive few see the potential conflict of interest and question the very idea of the agency. Thus, John Corry, a former media critic for the *Washington Times* wrote in the March 27, 1995, issue:

> Lost in all the noise about the peril to Big Bird and Barney is the indisputable fact that public broadcasting is part of the press, and the press is supposed to be independent of government. . . . The arguments about public broadcasting will remain, intractable and insoluble, so long as it stays on the dole.

Corry is right on target. If CPB, PBS, and NPR want artistic freedom and a license to present slanted news like the rest of the networks, then they will have to pay their own way. Otherwise, they will have to endure the ignominy of greater and greater scrutiny and control by the elected representatives of those who pay the bills.

Question #2. If the American taxpayers are footing the bill for these TV and radio broadcasts, then don't they have a right to expect that public television will be pleasing and attractive to the

**whole family — to Mom and Pop and Granny and
Little Susie, as well as to Long-haired Larry and
the members of his heavy-metal band?**

Of course, no one is arguing that Fred Smith of
Steubenville, Ohio, should be able to call the Corporation for Public Broadcasting and issue orders concerning tomorrow's programming. But Fred has every right
to insist that his wishes and tastes are represented on
"public" broadcasts. He also has the right to protest
programming that offends his tastes and attacks his
most sacred beliefs. After all, he's part of that "public;"
and after watching PBS for three weeks without sleeping, he can't find a single program he likes. What he
does find is what he regards as biased news reporting
and obscene programs about Black homosexuals.

Of course, those who run PBS and NPR shudder
at the very idea that the Freds of America should have
the right to look over their shoulder. After all, they
argue, the people who run these agencies are broadcast
professionals with a level of expertise that Fred couldn't
possibly match. By interfering, Fred would only lower
the quality of what's being offered to the general public
and stifle the enormous creativity that they believe is so
characteristic of public television and radio.

The answer to that objection is obvious: Maybe
Fred isn't an expert on television and radio production,
but he is something even more formidable — he is a
taxpayer, and taxpayers are paying the bills for CPB. So
they have a right to say what's done with their money,
as do the shareholders of any corporation.

But how can CPD, PBS, and NPR please both Fred and those Black homosexuals who thought that "Tongues Untied" was the greatest thing ever screened on any television network? And going back to question number 1, how can the liberal executives and producers at PBS and NPR exercise artistic freedom if a Republican Congress is monitoring everything they are doing with the intention of disciplining them if they offend any subcommittee member or his wife — or, for that matter, a substantial portion of the American people?

These questions have no satisfactory answers. And that fact is itself revealing. The truth should be obvious: Government should not be funding these activities. In matters of taste and public policy, the American people are perennially and hopelessly divided — more so than at any time in our history. Consequently, any political or social commentary is bound to seem biased to a large segment of the audience; and what seems within the bounds of good taste to one group will be highly offensive to another. The small group in charge has things its way, and — as John D. Rockefeller once said — "The public be damned."

To illustrate this point, consider some of the following examples of programming, collected by pro-family activist Robert Knight, and how they may have struck a more conservative cohort of viewers and listeners.

> • In July of 1994, an Akron, Ohio, mother reported that on the local PBS station, a pro-homosexual program,

"What If I'm Gay?" was being screened during morning hours, when preschoolers were watching. As a matter of fact, the show was aired right after "Kidsong TV" and right before "Sesame Street." When the distraught mother called the station, she was told "The quality of the program is unquestionable. It has good writing and production and is well thought out."

• The Independent Television Service (ITVS) — has received $38 million in public broadcasting funds to produce no more than nine hours of programming. One of their projects — a five-hour series called "Television Families" — was designed to focus on "tales of more or less dysfunctional families." Another ITVS project, "Terminal USA," is described in the ITVS newsletter as concerned with "wholly unwholesome folks" who "cram a lot of skeletons into their closet: drug abuse, homosexuality, teen pregnancy, elderly abuse, unemployment, and infidelity (with the pizza delivery boy) — all under one roof." The newsletter concludes by saying, "Unlike the absolute 'family values' of censorship-minded evangelicals, 'TV Families' values all kinds of families."

• In 1992 PBS aired "What Kids

Want to Know About Sex and Growing Up," a documentary produced by the Children's Television Workshop. Robert Knight's description: "The show was an attack on traditional family values in the guise of a pseudo-scientific presentation. ... The program contains graphic sexual information, aimed at children as young as eight years old. Children are encouraged to use condoms without being informed about high condom failure rates. Abstinence is only given a passing mention. Parents are nearly invisible, as are clergy and other adults who would normally articulate moral and familial ramifications of sexuality."

• Another product of Children's Television Workshop is *Sesame Street Parents Magazine,* which recently featured a column by Dr. Lawrence Balter in which he describes masturbation as a "tension-relieving activity that, much like hair twirling and thumb-sucking, serves to soothe and calm children. Masturbation can also help a child learn more about his body and help him develop positive attitudes toward sex. . . . Avoid telling your son that touching himself is 'not nice.' "

PBS and NPR promote the gay rights agenda

almost daily and with little or no attempt to feign objectivity. This militant advocacy has led producers and reporters to oversimplify complicated issues and to offend large segments of their audience.

• In 1994, shocked viewers saw the PBS miniseries, "Tales of the City," which celebrated homosexuality in San Francisco during the 1970s. Like many broadcasts dealing with homosexual themes, it contained nudity, obscenity, and other forms of vulgarity. It also caricatured normal families and portrayed homosexuals as superior human beings.

• Perhaps the most widely publicized of PBS's pro-homosexual programs, "Tongues Untied" was aired in 1991 and provoked an avalanche of protests from all over the country. In fact, over 100 PBS stations refused to carry the program. A "documentary" on Black homosexuals, which featured frontal nudity and, among other obscenities, depicted two men taking off their clothes and engaging in an unnatural sex act. These homo-erotic scenes were framed by flights of pompous rhetoric masquerading as poetry.

• A year later, PBS recognized "Gay Pride Month" by offering a film about a father and son both of whom come out of the closet and admit they are homosexuals. Like "Tongues Untied," the film contains explicit homo-erotic scenes.

Another characteristic of both PBS and NPR is their unabashed anti-religious bigotry. If the First Amendment means anything, it prohibits the federal government from oppressing or persecuting specific religious denominations. Yet this is precisely what government-subsidized radio and television are doing. Consider the following examples, only a few of the many that occur in PBS and NPR programming.

• In October of 1993, NPR aired a program designed to discredit conservative orthodox Christians who participate in politics. After decades of praising the involvement of clergy in the Civil Rights movement, "In Jesus' Name: The Politics of Bigotry" attacks the idea that people with religious convictions should try to influence public policy. This program is so filled with misrepresentations that it constitutes little more than a mean-spirited smear funded by U.S. taxpayers, some of whom belong to the very organizations depicted. The show ran two and one-half hours. Among the charges leveled against the "Christian right" — charges that Christians were not allowed to answer: "The Christian Right consists of] people who have a certain world view that they want to impose on the rest of society...." "The kid that graduated from their Christian schools voted for George Bush this year [laughs]. And the youngster that they enroll today will be voting for some other conservative and be just as bigoted 15 years from now." "Focus on the Family is a large and influential Christian Right ministry that hides behind a facade of being a social service agency." In the course of the broadcast, Christians are compared to Hitler, Nazis, and the Ku Klux Klan."

• Bill Moyers, in a show that has run on PBS for years, devoted a segment to "Amendment Two," the Colorado initiative to prohibit counties and municipalities from granting special rights and protections to homosexuals. Instead of giving a balanced account of the controversy, Moyers depicted orthodox Christians as bigots, while showing homosexuals as innocent victims of oppression. Moyers called this segment "The New Holy War" and suggested that the whole controversy was a product of religious fanaticism, when in fact a number of secular organizations and nonevangelicals supported the initiative.

In addition to the anti-religious bias, both PBS and NPR are laden with programs extolling the ideas and activities of the Left. While the phrase "radical right" is frequently heard on the public airways, the phrase "radical left" is never uttered. Indeed, left-wing leaders and organizations are show-cased in major programs, often presented as if their views were centrist and normative.

• In May of 1994, National Public Radio decided to feature convicted cop-killer former Black Panther Mumia Abu-Jamal in a series of commentaries. The publicly funded network explained this programming as an effort to "bring a unique perspective to listeners." After then-minority leader Robert Dole denounced CPB on the floor of the Senate, the project was quietly dropped — one of the few examples of prudence on the part of the corporation's leadership.

• NPR and PBS are constantly offering puff pieces on America's enemies. Whether El Salvador, Cuba, or Libya, nations and political factions that oppose the United States are given voice and sympathetic treatment.

• And public network reporters are people who wear their anti-American biases like buttonhole flowers, not only in NPR and PBS broadcasts, but also when appearing on other programs.

• Consider the blind animosity of reporter Sunni Khalid as expressed in this quote on events in Haiti: "I think there's a big difference when people told Father Aristide to sort of moderate his views, they were concerned about people being dragged in the streets, killed, and necklaced. I don't think that is what Newt Gingrich has in mind. I think he's looking at a more scientific, a more civil way, of lynching people."

These examples could be multiplied to flesh out an entire book on the subject of the virulent bias of NPR and PBS, a bias clearly alien to a majority of the American people. Of course, apologists for CPB will immediately point out that PBS and NPR put on a lot of programming that pro-family people enjoy: "Masterpiece Theater," concerts, Agatha Christie mysteries, and nature shows. But these bland and non-controversial programs don't make up for the aggressive promotion of leftist ideology, obscenity, and anti-American propaganda. The public is angry, and their anger will not subside.

Indeed, the escalation of this controversy can lead reasonable and fair-minded Americans to only one conclusion: the Corporation for Public Broadcasting must be cut loose from the apron strings of Big Government and allowed the absolute "freedom to offend" that the agency so obviously cherishes. Even Big Bird needs to grow wings and fly. At this moment in history, he needs to be kicked out of the nest and sent soaring into free sky, where he can go where he chooses and where there is a lot of competition for worms. Recently Ervin S. Duggan, the president of PBS, told a New York audience: "Commercialized public television is likely to resemble, for all the world, Thomas Hardy's ruined maid: 'no longer pure and simple, brazenly working the streets in her new commercial finery, doing whatever is necessary to survive.' " In addition to misreading cynical Hardy's poem — which actually suggests that the "ruined maid" is better off in her new life — Ervin's melodramatic comparison has offended members of Congress.

As Robert L. Livingston, Republican from Louisiana, put it: "I am appalled by the stupidity of Mr. Duggan's comments. They are so far removed from reality that he has convinced that his cause is not worthy of support by the United States taxpayers."

Welcome aboard our bandwagon, Congressman!

12

Fulfilling the Contract

These, then, are the 10 promises the Republican Party should make to pro-life, pro-family Americans. They are promises that can be kept because the majority of the American people believe in them. The ten initiatives don't call up the vision of a glorious but hypothetical future; they address the loss of a very real past. If offered and granted, they would simplify our lives rather than complicate them and save resources rather than cost more money than we can afford to pay.

If you think about it, you'll realize that most of these 10 promises do little more than abolish agencies that never should have been created, reverse decisions the Supreme Court never should have made, repeal programs that never should have been established, and set aside policies that never should have been adopted. All we ask is that the nation be restored to the health it enjoyed prior to the 1960s.

The Corporation for Public Broadcasting, the National Endowment for the Arts, the National Endowment for the Humanities, the Department of Education — all of these agencies have been created in the past 30 years and are little more than barnacles on the ship of state, expensive bureaucracies that insult the good sense and good taste of the American people. If they were abolished, no one would miss them except for the bureaucrats whose jobs would be eliminated and the hogs who feed at the trough of culture.

The 1962 prayer decision and the *Roe v. Wade* reveal a basic flaw in the Constitution, one the founding fathers couldn't have foreseen. Since they regarded the Supreme Court as little more than a forum in which to settle disputes between states, they could hardly have anticipated that with lifetime appointments and the Constitution itself as a perennial playtoy, in time the Court could become the one branch of government without an effective check, an oligarchy deciding the most important questions of the day in terms of their own private ideology. If the two constitutional amendments are passed by Congress and ultimately ratified, the people of the United States will have gone a long way toward humbling the High Court and informing its members that they, too, are finally fallible and accountable.

The repeal of Title X — an expensive exercise in futility — will be important for two reasons. First, it will save the taxpayers billions of dollars over the next few decades, when a few billion dollars may prove to be the difference between balancing the budget and sinking deeper into debt. But more important, the abolition of the program will defund some of the most vicious organizations and practices the government has ever supported. The corruption of the young and the serial killings of the unborn by such organizations as Planned Parenthood will be significantly diminished and perhaps in time completely eliminated. This certainly isn't the largest program in the government, but it may well be the most degenerate.

Finally, the funding of the Gay Rights movement and the admission of homosexuals into the military are policies that sicken the American people and lead them to believe that their government is finally without sense or principle — a vast bureaucracy that responds only to threats and intimidation. Americans are not key-whole peepers nor are they holier than thou. For generations homosexuals have lived peacefully and comfortably in communities all over the nation — until they began to bring their behavior and their warped vision of society to Main Stream America. The time has come for the Gay Rights movement to withdraw from the public eye and concentrate on reforming its behavior and policing the extremists in its own ranks. Homosexuals are not being persecuted in the United States of America — never have been, never will be. Last year, with gay rights publications begging homosexuals to report any kind of hate crime against them in order to run up the count, the FBI could only identify around 500 against gays — less than one per state per month. You can be certain that little old ladies are being attacked in about the same numbers — or any other identifiable group you could name.

So what we're trying to do in this Pro-Family Contract is to restore America, to help our nation become again what it once was — a nation rich in virtue as well as in dollars. This seems like an easy task, but in reality it will be extremely difficult. A number of vested interests are determined to block any kind of social reform, any step in the direction of what is wholesome and decent and pure — the liberal wing in Congress that created and voted for most of these things; the ideological organizations like People for the American way and the American Civil Liberties Union; the beneficiaries of the taxpayer's bounty — Planned Parenthood, the creators of trivial and obscene art, the teenager who made certain she got pregnant so the government would set her up in her own apartment; and the ideologues, those like Harry Blackmun who believe fiercely and mindlessly in their own vision of America — never mind what the nation has always been or what the people would like it to remain.

There is also another force at work to prevent reform, to prevent the new majority from shrinking government and repealing the mistakes of the past — a force at least as powerful as the old leadership in Congress or the rich and powerful organizations that have always run Washington. This force is the American press — which is monolithic in its support of Big Government and without scruples in the tactics it will use to sustain the status quo. With few exceptions, every major newspaper in the United States has an editorial position to the left of the American people and all five networks are pushing the social agenda of the 1960s, even as the American people are becoming disillusioned with political correctness.

A recent poll told the story: the overwhelming majority of the American people believe the nation is headed in the wrong direction — a whopping 69 percent. Indeed, only 24 percent believe we're moving in the right direction — an extraordinarily low level of confidence for a nation that has always been optimistic about itself and the future. Clearly the American dream has turned into a nightmare for an enormous portion of the population.

But there is a new spirit in the Congress — and particularly in the House — a spirit that is unafraid of controversy and eager to set things right. There are also millions of Americans who hope to see this second Contract fulfilled, who believe in it even more than they believed in the first Contract, and who are willing to become involved politically for the first time in their lives. Both of these groups need to organize themselves in order to address these problems and to become aggressive in support of traditional family values. Here is a suggested agenda for each group.

A Game Plan for Congress to Pass the Pro-Family Contract

1. Members of Congress must begin to speak out on the social issues.

Given the importance of the social issues, it is important that members of Congress begin to discuss such controversial topics as abortion, gay rights, obscene art, the history standards, and teenage pregnancy. Obviously, the opposition has no qualms about bringing these issues before the American people and giving them a politically correct "spin." Gay rights is a good example. Homosexual activists have been all over the airways, all over the television screen, all over the pages of the newspapers — pushing their issues, making people listen to their arguments, insisting that theirs is the only right and compassionate position. Meanwhile, those members of Congress who believe in traditional values have been relatively silent, preferring to talk about other matters — the deficit, the tax cut, term limits.

These people are our political leaders; the time has come for them to lead. If they don't have the courage to do so, then they should step aside and let others take their place. We need voices in Washington who will not merely mumble pro-life, pro-family sentiments behind closed doors but will speak them loudly and clearly in the halls of Congress, over the national radio and television networks, and on podiums around the country.

At the moment, only a few members of Congress are outspoken on the social issues, and they are constantly being pilloried in the press. If those who have remained silent will raise their voices, then these bold few will no longer seem so isolated or so at odds with the rest of Congress. The American people will quickly join a genuine movement to restore decency and morality to the nation. Polls continue to reveal that Americans are conservative on the social issues. They do not favor abortion on demand or gay marriages or allowing artists to receive federal funding for obscenity or government attacks on religion. They are ready to rally behind parties and candidates who stand for traditional values, but the leadership must begin to give voice to the concerns of pro-family America — and soon. If Republicans don't speak out for decency and morality and family and life — and don't do so immediately — then someone else surely will.

2. Conservative members of Congress should join the newly formed pro-family, pro-life caucus to pass this agenda and to promote pro-family, pro-life initiatives in the future.

Many legislative caucuses now exist within Congress to promote certain agendas and to generate specific kinds of legislation. The Black Caucus has been one of the most active and successful, but there have been others organized to support specific industries and economic interests, in particular states or districts. Recently a pro-family caucus was organized to push for the wide range of legislative initiatives necessary to protect family life and values in the nation. Since many of the policies of the federal government have been actively anti-family for the past few years, much needs to be done: Laws must be repealed, federal regulations rewritten, agencies and offices redefined or eliminated.

A permanent caucus dedicated to pro-family issues can donate staff time for the creation of a pro-family agenda for the twenty-first century. Such an agenda should initially involve the undoing of damage inflicted by the Congress and courts for a period of some 40 years, but eventually it could also focus on constructive action that could be taken to ensure that a consortium of Planned Parenthood, the Human Rights Campaign, and the National Organization of Women won't initiate new legislation in the future to disrupt and subvert American family life.

3. Support the Pro-Family Contract with America, make sure that its provisions come to the floor, and then vote for every single item.

The passage of the Contract with America has helped to renew the faith of the American people in their political institutions, and several of the bills passed will have far-reaching effects on the nation's future. But that future is by no means assured — not when more than a million of the nation's unborn are killed annually, when the Gay Rights movement is influencing what our students are taught about sexuality in schools, when the government is funding obscenity in the arts and on radio and television, when children are told they can't say prayers during school lunch, when tax payers are subsidizing and therefore encouraging illegitimacy, and when our military strength is undermined by perverse social engineering. If these trends continue — if Congress is willing to allow these assaults on traditional morality and our innate sense of decency — then economic reforms will ultimately prove inadequate to prevent our ultimate decline and fall.

With the new crop of freshmen in Congress — and with most of these issues already introduced as legislation in the 104th Congress — we have the possibility of keeping each of these promises. Sure, it will be difficult to override a presidential veto on many of these issues. But these will be only temporary losses, a beginning for an agenda that will have a long shelf life in the hearts of the American people. Besides, it is important to get the bills on the floor, allow the public to see and hear the debate, and then make each and every member of Congress take a stand. The liberal Democratic leadership has been able to obscure their party's stance on family issues for years by refusing to let potentially popular pro-family legislation out of committee. A vote on such matters as federal funding for gay rights groups and school prayer will allow the public to see who supports family values and who does not.

At that point — when all these issues are presented for an up-or-down vote — we will begin to know precisely where we stand: how far we've come, how far we still have to travel. And we will also learn a great deal more about how the American people really feel about questions of public decency and morality.

In addition to the necessity for congressional action, it's also important that the pro-family community in America rise to the occasion and take an active role in the promotion and passage of the Pro-Family Contract with America. There are several actions that groups and individuals can take to ensure the success of this agenda, strategies that should be initiated immediately.

1. Pro-family advocates throughout the United States should write or call their U.S. representative and senators, insisting that they support and vote for the Pro-Family Contract with America.

Anyone familiar with the way Washington works knows that no lobbyist, however aggressive and well-funded, can compete with an aroused constituency that makes its wishes known. No member of Congress will risk alienating a large segment of his constituency for a trip to the Bahamas or dinner and champagne at the Hay-Adams — or even for a maximum contribution to his re-election campaign. Members of Congress know that they must please the folks back home if they hope to return to Washington. If they think the voters feel strongly about a particular issue, then they will go out of their way to remain in the good graces of the electorate — even at the risk of missing a few good dinners and trips with their favorite lobbyists.

Of course, the people who lobby against the best interests of American families are more likely to approach members with misleading statistics (including public opinion polls) and threats of reprisal. Homosexual lobbyists claim to represent 10 percent of the population. Feminist groups claim to represent all women. Abortion advocates cite carefully worded polls that suggest an overwhelming number of Americans favor abortion on demand. These claims are all outrageous, and they can only be answered by a strong grassroots showing on the part of pro-family groups and individuals nationwide.

If you are a constituent and want to make your voice heard, here are some suggestions about making contact with your two senators and your U.S. representative.

1. Write and say that you support the entire Pro-Family Contract with America and expect them to do so as well.

Here are some pointers to follow in drafting such a letter.

• Be brief and direct in what you say. Don't try to argue the points at great length, unless you bring some special expertise to an item (e.g., an obstetrician who opposes abortion). In most cases, congressional staff members have briefed the senator or representative on the issue, pro and con. Assume that the congressional office knows the basic arguments. What you want to accomplish is to let them understand precisely which points are most important to you.

• Be courteous. If you sound too belligerent or mean-spirited, the staff will assume you are a crank and dismiss your opinion. This will mean that your letter will not be among those passed along to the member.

• On the other hand, make certain that you convey the full measure of your support for this Pro-Family Contract. It's perfectly acceptable to use phrases like: "I feel very strongly about this issue" or "I will regard this vote as an indication of whether or not you share my values and beliefs." But always end your letter with a friendly closing. Good people can disagree on some of these issues.

• If you are a member of a church or civic club whose members tend to support the Contract, you should certainly feel free to say, "Almost everybody in our church [or club] believes the Pro-Family Contract should be passed in its entirety." If you are an officer or leader of such a group, be sure to say so.

• If you wish, you can include some prepared literature on the Contract or on the individual issues. It will give your elected representative some idea of who is influencing the opinions of people in the state or district.

• When you receive a reply — and it's highly unlikely that you won't — study it very carefully. Most congressional offices are highly skilled in crafting replies designed to lead you to believe the senator or representative agrees with the opinions you've expressed in your letter. Sometimes the reply will focus on only one point you have made. "I notice that you are opposed to funding for the Gay Rights movement. I have always voted against such funding. For example, two years ago. . . ." Sometimes the member will respond with vague generalities: "I, too, believe that the family is the most important institution in our society and I will continue to support legislation that furthers the interest of our families." It's surprising how many constituents are satisfied with such evasive answers and never bother to check on how the senator or representative subsequently voted on the bill in question.

• Don't believe you're wasting time when you write a letter to your senator or congressman. What you write will be read and carefully considered,

provided it is serious and observes the
rules of common courtesy.

2. Get your friends to write.

You can multiply your influence by persuading
friends and family members to write a letter as well.
Again, don't ask them merely to repeat the same words
you've written. Make certain they give their own
thoughts in their own language. But be sure and tell
them that (1) their letter will be read and answered and
that (2) congressional offices know that a few letters on
an issue represent thousands of like-minded people
who don't take the time to pass along their thoughts.

3. Call the office of your representative or state office of your senator and state your concerns to the staff member in charge of the issue.

Again, there's no need to spend a lot of time
arguing the case. The fact that you've called is evidence
enough that you are concerned about this issue. The
phone will probably be answered by a receptionist who
will refer your call to someone qualified to answer your
questions or discuss your comments. When the receptionist answers, "Senator Washington's office," simply
say, "I'd like to speak to someone about the Pro-Family
Contract with America."

Get to the point immediately. Say something
like, "I'm calling in support of the Pro-Family Contract
with America." Then make sure that whoever takes

your call — probably a legislative assistant — understands exactly how you feel about the Contract and why you support it. You might want to jot down a few notes before you make the call, just so you remember every important point and at the same time don't ramble on. When you've made your points, say, "That's all I want to say. I appreciate your time. I hope you'll pass along my thoughts to the senator." And the legislative assistant might just do that — if you sound sincere and intelligent.

By the way, don't forget that U.S. representatives have district offices and senators have state offices, usually in more than one city. Many members of Congress and their staffs believe that the district offices have a better grasp of grassroots sentiment than the Washington office, which is too often crowded with lobbyists, the staff members of other elected officials, and people looking for support for their pet projects. So you might want to call the district or state office and in the process save yourself a few bucks.

4. Write letters to your local newspaper, giving reasons why the Pro-Family Contract with America should be enacted into law.

You'd be surprised at the number of people who read the "Letters to the Editor" section of the newspaper and are influenced by what they see there. Those who run this department are always looking for intelligent letters on controversial subjects. The letter should be thoughtful and informative, though by no means timid.

Remember that a majority of the readers probably don't have a strong opinion on this subject, and your letter may be just what they need to make up their mind and call their congressman. Remember, as well, that most congressional offices employ "clipping services," which send them stories and comments about public policy. Many of these services clip letters from the editor as well as columns and editorial comment.

5. Call radio talk shows and express your opinion on the subject of the Pro-Family Contract.

One of the most important political developments in recent years has been the growing influence of talk radio on the attitudes and voting habits of Americans. Many Democrats blame their 1994 loss of the House and the Senate on Rush Limbaugh, and some have even proposed legislation to drive him off the air or else require stations to give commentators with opposing points of view equal time. These are the same Democrats, I might add, who turn a deaf ear to complaints that NPR and PBS display a leftist bias, despite the fact that tax dollars are being used to fund public radio and television, while Rush Limbaugh and the stations who carry him have to earn their way in the marketplace of ideas.

Whether or not Rush Limbaugh was single-handedly responsible for the GOP victory in November of 1994, it is certainly true that talk radio has awakened millions of Americans to the realities of contemporary politics and influenced a number of people in their thinking about current issues. Virtually every city and town in the nation has access to such radio programs, and you can be certain that the Pro-Family Contract with America will be a hot topic of conversation on such shows in the immediate future.

If you want to promote the Contract, then muster your arguments, find a talk show on your dial, and join in the dialogue. Some hosts and stations will be sympathetic with your support. Others will be hostile. You must decide whether you're the kind of person who avoids conflict or thrives on it, then choose your talk show accordingly.

6. Speak at local service clubs.

Everyone is not a public speaker; and if the idea terrifies you, put it out of your mind. However, if you like to perform before an audience, you might put together some remarks on the Pro-Family Contract with America and find one of the local service organizations that allows speeches on political topics. Some do and some don't. You'll just have to ask. If you'd like a prepared speech on the subject or talking points, write the Christian Action Network at the following address, enclose a stamped, self-addressed envelope, and C.A.N. will furnish you with one or both of these items.

Christian Action Network
P.O. Box 206
Forest, VA 24551

7. Collect and distribute literature on the subject.

As the Pro-Family Contract with America becomes a topic of conversation nationwide, newspapers and journals of opinion will be analyzing its provisions and taking a stand for and against its passage. Everyone interested in promoting the Contract can gather published arguments that support the pro-family agenda, reproduce them, and make them available to churches, civic centers, neighbors, and friends. If this contract is fulfilled, the process will be lengthy and filled with conflict. The television networks and major newspapers will be opposed to most, if not all, of its provisions. The American people must be given sufficient information to understand the issues involved and speak out in behalf of this ten-point reform movement — even if that information must be passed along from hand to hand by people like you.

8. Join a political organization that supports family values and make yourself a part of an organized effort to promote this legislation and to elect candidates who believe in the Pro-Family Contract.

The most obvious organization to join is a political party and in many places the most obvious party to join may be the GOP. Over the past few years, Republicans have tended to nominate many more pro-family, pro-life candidates than the Democratic Party. It's perhaps significant that the Republican national platform for the past four elections has contained a strong, pro-life plank. Indeed, the Democratic Party refused to allow Governor Casey of Pennsylvania to speak before their last convention because he is pro-life.

On the other hand, in some locales Republican leaders are by no means either pro-life or pro-family. In 1990, for example, Pennsylvania Republicans nominated a pro-abortion candidate for governor to run against a pro-life Democrat. And in 1994, that same GOP nominated a man who was both pro-abortion and pro-gay-rights. So you should be careful to investigate the local party before you pay your dues and join. No one should waste energy and money supporting the candidacy of Tweedledum, even if Tweedledee belongs to the more liberal of the two national parties.

Participating in partisan politics can be very rewarding, particularly in times like these, when the lines are so clearly drawn. Once you are a member of a political party, you should use your influence to persuade the local and state party organizations to urge House and Senate members to support the Pro-Family Contract. Continued party support is very important to elected officials. Many of their volunteers and a substantial portion of their funding come from the party, and they can't afford to alienate such organizations. If they really believed they would lose party support by voting against the Contract, they would think long and hard before bucking their own base of support.

Of course, if you don't like party politics or your local leadership, there are other grassroots organizations that are actively involved in influencing local, state, and national elections. Some of these are religious-oriented groups. Others are purely secular. A few make a real difference in the political arena.

Make certain, however, that you know what kind of group you're joining before you sign aboard. You don't want to be associated with an organization that advocates extra-legal tactics, condones violence, or subscribes to disreputable attitudes. In other words, you want to ascertain precisely what principles the organization upholds, not only publicly, but also privately. In most cases, of course, you can reassure yourself without too much trouble.

9. You can pray.

A few years ago I read about a clergyman in a small town who had just run a successful campaign to remove pornographic materials from a small chain of convenience stores in his rural area. He talked about the tactics he and his congregation had used: friendly warnings, sermons on Sunday, a quiet boycott — and prayer.

"I don't think you could overestimate the role of prayer in this victory," he said. "We believe it was the single most important factor in changing the minds of these people."

The same may be true of the Pro-Family Contract for America. At the beginning of this fight, with the vast forces of secularism lined up against us, we earnestly solicit your prayers. With a strong and active new Congress, with thousands of grassroots supporters, and with the blessings of God, we can win this late, great battle for the soul of our nation.

Notes

[1]Martin Mawyer, *Silent Shame: The Alarming Rise of Child Sexual Abuse and How to Protect Your Children From It* (Wheaton, IL: Crossway Books, 1987).

[2]Dr. Paul Cameron, *The Gay Nineties* (Franklin, TN: Adroit Press, 1993), page 126.

IT'S HOT!

Get THREE FREE issues of the

WASHINGTON HOTLINE

Find out what Congress is doing with the
Pro-Family Contract with America!

Get your 3 free issues of CAN's **Washington Hotline** newsletter just by completing this form and returning it to the address below. No obligations. No hassles. Just a lot of good, solid news you won't find anywhere else!

The **WASHINGTON HOTLINE** is a publication of the Christian Action Network and provides readers with an exclusive, insider's view of what is happening in Congress. And not only does it inform you of the latest news on the Pro-Family Contract, it also keeps you abreast of other critical developments in our nation's Capitol.

To get your 3 complimentary issues of the HOT-TEST newsletter about Washington, please complete the form below and return it as soon as possible.

Name_____

Address _____

City_____State____Zip _____

❏ Please check this box to receive a 1 year subscription, along with your 3 FREE issues to the **Washington Hotline**, for $24.95.

Please mail this completed form to

Christian Action Network • P.O. Box 606 • Forest, VA 24551